THE LAND OF WHITE

ABOUT THE AUTHOR

Lina Saad was born in Sierra Leone, West Africa. During the 1980s Lina attended Evangelical School in Beirut and lived through the Civil War, experiencing the severe stress the Lebanese went through at this time. In 1986, she joined her parents back in Sierra Leone until she completed her GCEs and then returned to Lebanon to graduate from high school. Lina graduated from Westminster College with a BA (Hons) in Hotel Management and established Alicia Restaurant in Warren Street, London.

LINA SAAD

The Land of White
Simple Lebanese Cookery

A CIP catalogue record for this title is available from the British Library.

ISBN 978-1-78612-473-9 (paperback)
ISBN 978-1-78612-474-6 (hardback)

www.austinmacauley.com

First Published (2015)
Austin Macauley Publishers Ltd.
25 Canada Square
Canary Wharf
London
E14 5LQ

Printed and bound in Great Britain

This book is dedicated:

To my husband Dr Ali Saad and our two lovely, supportive children
Hsein and Lameece.

To my aunt Samia who brought me up since I was 18 months and taught me
the love of food and cookery.

To my Mum and Dad, thank you for your continued support in the journey of
food romance – especially the indulgent desserts Mum always makes for us.

CONTENTS

Introduction

I BELIEVE WE ARE always nostalgic about our childhood stories, habits and memories. We pile them up as we go further in our lives; the haunting memories keep popping up until we relive them with our kids or share them with friends and loved ones.

Picture taken by myself!
*You can see the **El Rawshe Rocks**: a breathtaking sight.*

My most perfect memory is landing at Beirut airport early in the morning – about 5 a.m. – and hitting the streets of this vibrant and ever-noisy city to buy Manakeesh, round dough topped with zaatar mix or cheese and sesame seeds, then rolling to Al Hamra or Verdun (different reputable streets for shopping, equivalent to Knightsbridge and Oxford Street in London) to buy Kaaket Kunafa, a round mini-bread stuffed with a dessert made of sweet white cheese and a special pastry known as 'Shaar', all drizzled with sugar syrup.

Sawda Naye and Liyee, fresh raw liver with diced pieces of fat enjoyed as they are with seven spices – a Lebanese specialty combining cumin, paprika, coriander, nutmeg, cloves, cinnamon and black pepper – salt, sweet white onions and fresh mint.

By the time I get home at about 7 am, I am already surrounded by my loving family and a huge table full of heavenly, mouthwatering breakfasts. My aunt has brought the fresh raw liver from her trusted local butcher – she would have reserved this liver two days before – with some lovely crisp vegetables, like spring onions, white onions and fresh mint leaves, beside it. My uncle has got us some Foul Modamas and Balila; the former is fava beans and chickpeas cooked with garlic, lemon juice and olive oil, and the latter is just chickpeas that are heavily cooked until they can be semi-mashed, which is slightly creamier in texture than the first. This is also cooked with garlic, olive oil and lemon juice. Usually these are served with pickled turnips, chillies and cucumbers as well as fresh vegetables such as onions, tomatoes, radish and fresh mint. They are sold by the local shops known as 'Fawal' who only serve cooked and pureed pulses like 'Fatet Humus', 'Humus Puree', 'Foul' and 'Balila'.

Balila: this is when the chickpeas are cooked thoroughly until they become creamy with lemon juice, garlic and olive oil) and some Manakeesh Zaatar.

My other uncle had decided to go to Burj Hamood; this is where the famous Armenian souks and shops are. Most of them are great butchers and renowned for their 'Basturma' and varied spicy sausages or 'Sujuk'.

'*Basturma*', a cured meat, is a highly seasoned and air-dried beef of Armenian and Ottoman origins, introduced to Lebanon and Syria through the Armenian Diaspora during Ottoman rule. The history of '*Basturma*' goes back to the Byzantine period when cured meats were made in huge numbers in Anatolia.

My uncle also brings us '*Sujuk*' and '*Makanek*' and these are just delicious spicy sausages with pine kernels. All one has to do is cut them in the middle and cook in a dash of oil, lemon juice, salt and pomegranate molasses.

The picture above shows 'Tarboush', a biscuit with marshmallow cream, dressed with chocolate. As a child I loved this confectionery; my aunt used to give me 3 Lebanese Liras as a daily allowance and I had to spare 25 cents on this 'Tarboush'. I am so pleased I can still buy it in England from Sweetland's store in Park Royal and share it with my kids.

Cooking is part of our daily routine whether we like it or not. Recently, everyone is getting into this great activity using a million different ingredients and cookery methods, whether to satisfy basic needs or to feed a crowd – or even just to satisfy their greedy indulgence!

When I first thought of sharing my Lebanese recipes with a European audience, it happened that many people hugely enjoyed this cuisine and read about it, but never managed to get their 'hands wet' actually making the food. I must agree, it is often not easy to work with ingredients and cookery methods that are different to one's culture, but this combination of recipes is designed to make you just do it.

All the recipes should be doable from the comfort of your kitchen. Most of the ingredients are easily available in Middle Eastern shops, which can now be found not only on London's famous Edgware Road, but in towns and cities all over the UK.

The edition does not only get your hands wet and tongue tantalized, it will definitely transport you to the origin of the country's shared dishes and increase your insight into the Lebanon. If you follow the recipes step by step you are guaranteed to enjoy cooking as well as eating Lebanese style with a twist.

It is absolutely fun to get your kids involved in crushing the garlic using a pestle and mortar; it is definitely exercise for my little Hsein! And how about making baba ganouj at home, cutting through a pomegranate and tapping the seeds out? It is certainly exciting to enjoy crispy yet succulent grilled chicken thighs bursting with flavours of the Mediterranean.

Introduce your palette to stuffed Swiss chard with lemon juice and olive oil. Love the rice pudding with fresh strawberry syrup made with fruit straight from my garden; the kids loved mashing the strawberries with a hand-held blender.

All in all, I hope you enjoy reading and cooking for as long as this book is in your kitchen. Have fun – and Keeeppp COOOOKING!

The Food of Lebanon

Lebanese food is often described as the jewel of the entire Middle Eastern cuisine. It is an ongoing, eclectic cuisine with non-stop varieties derived from the recipe itself or from its leftovers.

Lebanon is a small country with an important strategic position within the Middle East. Its history goes back to Phoenician times in 3000BC. The Greeks called it Phoenicia ('the purple place') due to the discovery on the Lebanese coastline of the murex mollusc with its purple dye.

The Phoenicians went on to become the first international traders. They sailed to many different countries and traded preserved foods, pulses and their famous wine, which was known as the wine of the kings.

Until today Lebanon has seen many invaders, the first of whom were the Canaanites (later known as Phoenicians). The other long-term invaders were the Egyptians who ruled for three hundred centuries from 1484 to 1150BC. The Lebanon was then invaded by the Assyrians, followed by the Babylonians, the Persians, the Macedonians under Alexander the Great and, of course, the Romans. Finally, the Ottomans spread their rule over the country, starting in 1516 AD when Syria and Lebanon were just one country. Post World War I Lebanon, as part of the former Ottoman Empire, became a French Mandate, 1920–1946.

The above factors are the major influence on the highly eclectic nature of Lebanese cuisine. In addition, Lebanon is blessed with four distinct seasons and many waterfalls; above all, its soil, the famous *terra rossa*, is ideal for any plantation and a variety of agricultural produce, especially wines.

The Lebanese start their meals with mezze which is a selection of starters served hot or cold. It depends on the occasion but many people enjoy these starters for up to four hours.

Memoirs of the Golden Days

'My Grandfather and uncles asked the waiter for a bottle of locally made arack (raki) – this is a cloudy, alcoholic drink with a strong flavour of aniseed. They then started throwing in endless platters of mezze: tabbouleh, fatoush, humus, baba ganouj, vine leaves, kibbe balls, raw kibbe, raw frake, raw liver and fat that goes very well with arack. It has always been an amazing gastronomic experience.

The best of all, though, is the traditional oval fresh vegetable platter (a combination of cos/romaine lettuce, extra large beef tomatoes, a couple of mini-cucumbers, green peppers and some carrots), all to crunch on until the mezze starts. Other dishes are also thrown in during this time, like savoury spinach doughs, sambousek with meat or cheese, shankleesh and much more. About two hours later and depending on the location of the restaurant we then eat fried or grilled fish or even grilled lamb and chicken. I remember going to 'El Berdawne' in Zahle, eastern Lebanon, because it was famous for fish dishes like sea bass and trout: these are farmed nowadays but not in my day. The waiters threw in large oval dishes of deep-fried sardines and deep-fried pitta bread all with tahini and herbs sauce. All I had to do as a child was grab things and put them in my mouth and *Jedo Abou Sami* (my grandfather) just helped me do that. He took the sea bass and opened it in the middle to debone it and put

the pieces straight into my mouth with some tarator (tahini sauce with scallions and parsley).'

Such a cuisine highlights the cultural behaviour of the Lebanese where food is concerned, reminding us what once was said by the King of Assyria when he resided in the Land of White:

'Passerby, eat, drink and be merry, because the rest is worthless.'

This insight into the cultural aspects of Lebanese food is still the same as it used to be thousands and thousands years ago. Despite the political conflicts happening today, we still unite at one table and enjoy our national mezze and drink to our food heritage.

The photograph opposite shows olives mixed with garlic, walnuts and chillies; baby aubergine pickled with walnut and garlic stuffing; and plate of strained yoghurt. This is a typical breakfast popular in the region of Baalbeck, known as the 'Sun City', where the Romans resided and where their buildings survive as ruins. Baalbeck is located in the Eastern part of Lebanon, further away from the famous fertile flat land of the Bekaa Valley. The latter is famous for its high-quality terra rossa soil and where the sun is 90 degrees, resulting in the best wines in the world. The Lebanese wines are renowned and highly reputed by many world experts; brands such as Ksara and Chateau Musar are among the most elite wines one can get hold of.

Despite the Ottomans' influence, the French mandate left the Lebanese with patisseries and croissants and baguette bakeries. They are all specialist shops; in '*Rass El Nabee*', where I was brought up and I still stay on my holidays, a Syrian gentleman who escaped Ottoman rule and resided in Beirut established a croissant shop. Many times before going to school my grandfather would buy me one with cheese or zaatar and I was allowed a chocolate croissant on the weekend.

Croissants recreated at home in London

Croissants with zaatar mix and with chocolate

DRINKS

THE MOST COMMON drinks in Lebanon are the Jallab and Tamarind. The former combines dates and grape syrup diluted with water and is served with crushed ice and pine nuts. Tamarind is the sweet syrup of the tamarind fruit, also diluted with water and served with nothing more than crushed ice. Other countries also favour Amaredine, a fruity concoction of sliced apricots, melted in water and sugar.

Milky Dates

'These are heavenly: the lovely contrast between cold, unsweetened milk and sweet and juicy dates. Pretty irresistible!'

This is definitely one of my favourite daily appetisers. Absolutely refreshing, sweet and nutritious, it's a simple must-have throughout summer and a great energizer to start your day.

You may use any type of dates, but my favourites are the large mejdool ones: they are sweet, plump and juicy. Place them in your desired glasses, take the seeds out and pour some cold milk over. I usually put one date in a shot glass or three in a larger glass. Leave in the fridge for a minimum of three hours.

Minty Lemonade

Known for its agricultural produce, the Lebanon is particularly famous for its citrus fruits. Lemons, pomellos and oranges are extremely popular; I recall very few recipes that do not incorporate citrus juice. For the summer afternoon, lemon juice infused with sugar, orange blossom and rose water with some mint leaves is an absolute heavenly experience!

Ingredients

10 lemons peeled, cut quarterly and deseeded

1.5 cup caster sugar (you may need to adjust the sugar according to your taste)

2 tbsp blossom water

1 tbsp rose water

1 litre water

Fresh mint leaves – a good handful

Ice cubes as desired

Put the ingredients into a blender and give it all a blitz.

Rose Water

Roses are symbol of love and peaceful messages to the receiver. It has been popular to use roses in many home made remedies throughout many centuries and it has proven to be a great therapy for rheumatism, asthma and its fragrances aids depression.

If we take into consideration the Aleppo Roses (they are best of quality and fragrance, Aleppo region in Syria), residents use these rose petals in many of their recipes and even their spice mixes and teas.

My grandmother loved rose syrup, she always prepared it in summer time and alongside many other fruit syrups such as Blackberry, Mulberry and pomegranate.

Rose syrup is widely available in many Middle Eastern shops in the UK; all you have to do is dilute with some cold water and a couple of ice cubes and – booom! – you are in absolute refreshing state of karma.

Laban Ayran (straight yoghurt)

Just the thought of this drink brings back many dear memories. The natural yoghurt is mixed with salt and water and that's it!!!

Ayran is similar to the Iranian drink Lassi, though the latter is often mixed with sugar. Yoghurt drink is refreshing, cooling and especially popular with meat dishes or pasties. Every time I visit Beirut, I make sure I enjoy a lovely minced lamb pasty (Lahme Bil Ajeen) with Laban Ayran.

The recipe for the Ayran below is not of my creation; it does follow the same concept as mine, but is a little bit unique. A family friend who is a head chef for a top-notch Lebanese restaurant in the UK invited us for dinner throughout Ramadan (Holy Month); excitement is always in the air when someone invites me for dinner because I want to experience other, different culinary ideas to mine. Here is his green, buzzing recipe for Laban Ayran.

Ingredients

250g natural yoghurt
Half a cucumber, chopped
8 leaves fresh mint
1 leaf cos/romaine lettuce
1 tbsp salt
500ml tap water
Handful of ice cubes

Mix all ingredients in a smoothie maker and whizz until all smooth; enjoy it with rice, pasty or just on its own.

My version would have just included the yoghurt, water, fresh mint and salt; it is up to our individual taste. It is often preferable to keep recipes simple, as less is often more. However, I like changing and twisting some recipes around.

SOUPS

A S HEALTHY AS the Lebanese are in their food culture, soups are not a popular course. The Lebanese cuisine offers some popular ones but I believe that the extensive, uniquely rich variety of mezze destroyed the value of soups and their creative flavours. Professionals involved in Lebanese cuisine focused only on the mezzes and their presentation or in modernizing the recipes. While soup ingredients are rich, many recipes were derived from Europe.

I have decided to include only four recipes. I am sure there are many others but did not want to incorporate more as it is not purely traditional to eat soups in the Land of White.

I believe soups are for calmer settings and definitely not for a busy table full of such vibrant mezzes as raw liver cubes, mini spicy sausages, lamb patty with burghul (crushed wheat). We are talking about a buzzing food celebration, with vibrant colours bursting with flavours and ingredients.

Despite this, all food is good at home and every other Lebanese household all enjoyed these most popular soups.

Vegetable soup

You may choose this recipe either with lamb necks or go solo vegetarian. However, I will be sharing both methods.

Ingredients

4 necks of lamb (optional)
1 bunch of celery
1 large leek
4 carrots
3 potatoes
1 onion
1 large vine tomato
1 chicken stock
Salt and black pepper to taste
Knob of unsalted butter

Note: use a couple of cardamom seeds and cloves and a cinnamon stick to season the necks of lamb during the boiling process.

Method

1) Place the necks of lamb in a pan and cover with water. Bring to boil and cook for about an hour or until the meat is thoroughly done. Add a tsp of salt and black pepper, a couple of cardamoms and cloves.

2) In the meantime, wash all the vegetables thoroughly and chop them roughly.

3) In a separate pan, add the knob of butter on medium heat (gas mark 4) and start sweating the onions and leeks, followed by the rest of the vegetables.

4) Stir from time to time, adding the stock cube and some of the lamb necks' stock fluid.

5) Bring the liquid to boil, reduce heat to gas mark 2 and add the rest of the lamb stock and the lamb, or just water if taking the vegetable-only option.

6) Simmer for about half an hour, or until the vegetables are cooked, season with salt and black pepper according to taste.

7) You may either whizz this through with a hand-held blender together with the lamb pieces or leave it as it is and enjoy the sublime taste of cooked fresh vegetables. I often need to blend it, as my kids never like to see the meat in their soup. So 'God Bless Blenders'!

Lentil and Swiss Chard

This is a great soup to start a meal: it is nutritious and full of flavour. Lentils go very well with lemon juice, garlic and coriander; the Swiss chard adds a different dimension to this recipe. When I first arrived in the UK I could not find Swiss chard so my mother substituted it with fresh spinach. The soup is just fresh and beyond my description.

Ingredients

2 bunches of fresh Swiss chard

½ cup of brown lentils

2 Spanish onions

Juice of 3 lemons (save 1 lemon for extra at service)

Knob of unsalted butter

Sprinkle of ground cinnamon to taste

2 cloves of garlic, crushed

½ bunch of coriander, roughly chopped

Method

1) Wash the Swiss chard thoroughly and watch out for any excess soil, usually found in the stalks. Chop it roughly.

2) Peel the onions and slice into trenches.

3) Wash the lentils and watch out for any stones or grains.

4) In a pan, melt the butter and sauté the onions until translucent.

5) Add the Swiss chard and sweat all together.

6) Add the lentils and stir for about 5–10 minutes.

7) Add around 1 litre of boiling water.

8) Juice one lemon and add to the soup; let it simmer for about 20 minutes on low heat.

9) Crush the garlic and chop the coriander. Add them to the soup.

10) Let the soup simmer on low heat for another 25 minutes or until the lentils are tender.

11) Add salt and black pepper to taste.

Red Lentils and Minced Lamb

Ingredients

1 cup of red lentils

200g minced lamb

2 onions, finely chopped

2 mid sized potatoes, diced

2 tbsp butter

1.5 litres of water

½ tsp ground cumin added at the end

Salt and black pepper for seasoning

Method

1) Peel the onions, chop them roughly and put into a hot pan with the butter.

2) Dice the potatoes and add them to the onions and give them a stir from time to time.

3) Add the minced lamb to the potatoes and onions and give them a good stir for about 5 minutes. Reduce the heat gently and season with salt and pepper.

4) Add the red lentils and give them another stir. Add the water and let it simmer for at least 40 minutes.

5) Finally, season with the ground cumin, and hand-blend it with just couple of whizzes: you don't want it to be too coarse or too smooth but somewhere in the middle.

6) Serve the soup with some croutons or toasted pitta bread and a squeeze of lemon.

Lentils and Cumin Soup

Lentil soup is amongst the most popular soups in the Lebanon. Pulses and cumin were widely used by the Romans and Greeks. The Roman writer Apicius devoted several recipes for chickpeas and lentils in his cookery book. This food tends to be associated with the proletariat or the poor people; it is more street food than what you would have found at Graeco-Roman banquets. According to Herodotus in the book *Food in Antiquity*, the lentil was a major food of a Graeco-Scythian tribe, the Callipidae, who grew it along with grain, onions, leeks and millet.

The combination is very popular throughout the holy month of Ramadan because of its calming effects on the digestive system.

Ingredients

2 red onions, finely chopped

1 cup red lentils, washed

¼ cup of long grain rice

Knob of butter

Drizzle of olive oil

Salt to taste

1 tsp ground cinnamon

1 tsp ground cumin

Lemon wedge at service (optional)

Croutons or toasted arabic bread squares (optional)

1.5 litres of hot water

Method

1) Peel the onions and chop finely. In a hot pot add the knob of butter and the drizzle of olive oil.

2) Sweat the onions and give them a stir from time to time.

3) In the meantime wash the red lentils and the rice thoroughly, removing any impurities.

4) Add the grains into the onions and stir for about 5 minutes.

5) Add the hot water and bring to boil on medium heat.

6) About 10 minutes later, add the salt, ground cinnamon and cumin and let the soup simmer on low heat until the lentils are cooked. (You can test that with a spoon, usually within 30 minutes).

7) Allow to cool for about 30 minutes and blitz with your hand-held blender.

8) Serve with toasted Arabic bread or croutons and a squeeze of lemon or lime juice.

My aunt Samia buying fresh lettuce from El Jiyeh in Southern Lebanon, April 2013.

SALADS

THE LEBANESE CONSUME raw vegetables in their salads and other recipes. The region has a rich and wide selection of local produce such as parsley, spring onions, flat green beans, okra and tomatoes, and much more. In the mountains of Lebanon, people are known to eat fresh and raw wild endives and spring onions with just fried eggs; this clearly shows how widely fresh raw and crispy vegetables are used in this area and definitely differentiates it from the region as a whole which has a more Saharan climate. The availability of these vegetables is evidently reflected by the Lebanese table: one may easily end up eating more than 70 mezze dishes incorporating different textures and flavours.

Feta salad

Ingredients

200g feta cheese (preferably Bulgarian)

1 romaine lettuce

3 little cucumbers

2 large vine tomatoes

A couple of spring onion sprigs

A couple of chopped radishes

A couple of fresh mint sprigs

50g black olives, pitted/de-stoned

Pinch of salt

Pinch of dry mint

Method

1) Chop up all the vegetables and place in a bowl.
2) Dice the feta cheese and add the pieces to the vegetables, along with the black olives.
3) Season with a pinch of salt and dry mint.
4) Drizzle on some extra virgin olive oil.

Rahib ('The Priest')

This is a chargrilled aubergine salad with freshly and finely diced tomatoes, spring onion, cucumber, radish, mint and parsley, all mixed with crushed garlic, lime juice and extra virgin olive oil and some salt.

The lightness of this dish seduces you into having it on the table every time friends and family are over.

Ingredients

Serves 4–6

2 medium sized aubergines

2 beef tomatoes

1 bunch spring onions

2 Middle Eastern cucumbers, or half of the large ones

4 radishes

2-3 cloves garlic, crushed with a pinch of salt
(depending on your taste buds)

Juice of 2 limes

30ml extra virgin olive oil

Salt to taste

Method

1) Wash all the vegetables thoroughly, completely wrap the aubergines in silver foil and fork the foil all round to allow heat to penetrate. Place the aubergines on direct heat on the gas (medium to high) and let it grill. However, if you have a char-grill area use it as this will definitely enhance the flavour of the aubergine. Keep turning the aubergine from one side to the other, assuring it is cooking all around.

2) In the meantime, start dicing your vegetables and place them in a bowl, crush the garlic with a pinch of salt and add to the vegetables.

3) After 15 minutes the aubergines should be cooked, so allow them to cool and then peel the skin off and chop to mini dices, or however it is convenient to you: for example, my mum just pounds it until it is semi-mashed, while my father loves it diced as he enjoys chopping.

4) Add the aubergines to the vegetables, juice of lime and crushed garlic and olive oil, season with salt and mix together gently and just enjoy. Rahib can be eaten with Arabic bread, or on nice crustini seasoned with more olive oil or just on its own. The sky's the limit. It's so simple.

'The first time I ate Rahib was with my grandfather in the mountains of Lebanon, a summer day where he took us on a trip to visit the village of the great Lebanese author Jibran Khalil Jibran who was born, raised in the most gorgeous habitat of Bshari. The water springs were just pure, full of life and absolutely cold; the fruits just tasted different, more delicious and scrumptious. As for today, I doubt whether the fruits where really different or was it the whole ambience, but a child's tastebuds can already be highly developed and the experience cannot be mistaken.

'Our journey continued towards the restaurant; one of many located on the higher hills so that guests can view the uplifting scenery and smell the pine tree conifers. My grandfather ordered us a mezze and asked the lady to start pounding the lamb shoulder for raw kibbe and frake (lamb puree mixed with crushed wheat and cumin mix). I sat on his lap and he gave me a little Arabic bread with the rahib in my mouth: he said, "This is the food of the priest." During WWI under Ottoman rule, the Lebanese used to hide in the convent and the priest would combine all the fresh vegetables and aubergines to share with the refugees in the mountains of Lebanon. "Ehh my dear child, people had dignity and courage, that was our religion, despite our different beliefs, and we were very happy."'

Mighty Fatoush

Ingredients

Romaine lettuce

3 vine tomatoes

3 cucumbers

1 green pepper

1 red pepper

6 radishes

½ bunch of parsley

¼ bunch or fresh mint

1 bunch of spring onion

3 garlic cloves, peeled and crushed

Toasted pitta bread

Juice of a lemon

Pinch of sumac (Middle Eastern ground berries, tangy
  in taste)

3 drizzles of extra virgin olive oil

1 tsp pomegranate molasses

Salt to taste

Method

1) Wash all the fresh vegetables thoroughly.

2) Chop the lettuce, tomatoes, cucumbers, peppers and radishes.

3) Chop the parsley, mint leaves and spring onions all finely.

4) Cut the pitta bread to little squares and toast in the oven until golden brown.

5) Peel the garlic cloves and crush them, juice the lemon and add the olive oil and sumac.

6) Add the dressing to the fresh vegetables, mix with your hands, sprinkle the toasted bread on top.

Note: To make a bread bowl, split the Arabic bread in half and place each half into a round mould and place in the oven until toasted and crisp. Fill them in with the mixed fatoush and serve immediately.

Halloumi Salad

Grilled halloumi cheese served with sliced layers of vine tomatoes, black olives and fresh mint.

Halloumi is a Cypriot cheese and it's rather chewy and rubbery. It is one of those tough cheeses that tolerate heat and I believe its appeal lies in its texture more than in its simple milky taste. It is the most popular cheese consumed in the Lebanon.

I believe that halloumi cheese enjoys the highest market share of cheeses in the Lebanon. It is sold toasted in a baguette with cucumber and fresh mint, as fresh halloumi wraps or even grilled halloumi salad with poppy and sesame seeds that adds a crispy crunch to it.

Ingredients

1 pack of Cypriot halloumi
1 beef tomato
Couple of olives
1 tsp sesame seeds
30g butter

Method

1) Cut the halloumi into 2cm thick slices and put into a hot pan with a knob of butter.

2) Toss the halloumi for about a minute on each side, remove from pan and then let it rest on kitchen towel.

3) Place between tomato slices with some olives and sprinkle of sesame seeds and fresh mint.

'I recall my aunt making a lovely halloumi wrap for me to take to school alongside a baby cucumber that we picked on the weekend from our land in the village. My aunt carried on coaxing me to take it to school because it was fresh and tasty and will definitely make me taller and bigger.

In the evenings, my Grandfather would ask for a halloumi and honey baguette as this is scrumptious and tastes heavenly.'

Tabbouleh

As a mother of two active kids, my summer days may become long, lazy and full of house chores as well as funny accidents in the house. It is always easy to take the kids for a walk in the early evenings. People from the area who are doing the same often ask me where do I come from; the moment I say Lebanon, everyone jumps about – 'Oo, I love tabbouleh and falafels and baba ganouj!'

Tabbouleh is the national dish of Lebanon and every year competitions are held around many villages for the grandest tabbouleh. I am seriously talking about 30kg worth of this tantalizing salad, if not more. It is certainly a popular salad, with ingredients that speak out for themselves.

The word 'taboule' comes from the word 'tabli' – in other words, seasoning. The Levant or the mountains of Lebanon were rich with herbs and cracked wheat. Even the Romans mentioned that Lebanon is rich with more than 3,000 edible herbs and bushy greens. It is likely that parsley, onions and mint were used as a seasoning for meat, as the combination is usually served with chargrilled Kafta (minced lamb, onions, parsley and seasoning) and has evolved to become finer chopped and served with burghul (cracked wheat) with a squeeze of lemon juice and olive oil. The region has gone through many political conflicts and people have different tastes and cooking experiments and the result we have inherited is incredible.

> 'My aunt would take me out on long walks, from the southern village of JBAA to Ein Qana, to pick fresh spring onions and parsley from her best friend's garden. We then all come back and they chop the herbs and tomatoes and squeeze that fresh lemon, to give me the best tabbouleh my taste buds ever had.'

Ingredients

1 bunch of parsley

1 bunch spring onions

5 sprigs of fresh mint (take mint leaves off)

3 vine tomatoes

30g white burghul (crushed wheat), soaked in water to become soft

Juice of one lemon

1 tsp salt

1 tsp pomegranate molasses

½ tsp ground cinnamon

Drizzles of extra virgin olive oil

Method

1) Chop all the vegetables finely.

2) Mix the dressing ingredients (juice of lemon, olive oil, pomegranate molasses, salt and ground cinnamon).

3) Mix with your hands and serve with fresh cos/romaine lettuce.

Laban bil Khiyar

This is a cool starter dip or a salad: the combination is always enjoyed in the summer with dry dishes such as lentils with rice, rice with minced lamb or even just on its own.

Ingredients

500g natural yoghurt

3 little cucumbers or ¾ of a large one

4 cloves of garlic, peeled and chopped

½ cup of cold tap water

Salt to taste

Sprinkle of dry mint (for the top)

Drizzle of olive oil (for the top)

Method

1) Pour the yoghurt into a bowl.
2) Wash the cucumbers thoroughly and dice them.
3) Peel the garlic cloves and crush them with a pinch of salt.
4) Add the cucumbers, crushed garlic and water.
5) Give them a bit of a stir, salt to taste.
6) Sprinkle the dry mint and drizzle of olive oil on top.

Salatet Addas Bil Hamud

This red lentil salad is one of my favourite dishes; it is so earthy and packed with flavour. Red lentils are one of those pulses which if combined with lemon juice and olive oil you can't stop eating! This salad is native to the mountains of Lebanon and also the southern region, where there is a relative reliance on pulses in the absence of meat; especially during those exceptionally cold winters when the roads are snow-blocked and not safe to use.

Ingredients

250g red lentils

1 aubergine, washed, peeled and sliced into 2cm pieces

Juice of 2 lemons

3 garlic cloves crushed

30ml extra virgin olive oil

Salt to taste

1 pomegranate (semi-sweet)

Oil for deep-frying

Method

1) Rinse the red lentils thoroughly and remove any extra stones or other impurities. Bring to boil in about 1 litre of cold water until tender. This may take up to 45 minutes.

2) In the meantime, peel the aubergine and slice into a 2cm thickness, season with salt and let it rest for about 20 minutes to reduce its moisture.

3) In a pan prepare 300ml vegetable oil for deep-frying. Pat each aubergine slice with a kitchen towel and fry on both sides until light golden. Then set aside on kitchen towel to drain excess oil.

4) Peel the garlic cloves and crush. Juice the lemon and mix with olive oil and the crushed garlic and leave aside.

5) The lentils should be ready by now, so pour out into a sieve and give them a gentle stir with a fork. Allow to cool then place in your desired dish and gently mix in the lemon and garlic dressing. Serve on a plate with some pomegranate rubies and couple of aubergine slices.

Avocado Salad

When reading you may ask what the avocado's relationship is with Lebanese cuisine. As mentioned earlier, the Land of White's collective cuisine is a result of all the many and varied cultures that ruled it. Many of the Lebanese also fled to Brazil and Africa. As a matter of fact my great grandfather and grandfather migrated to Brazil on a boat but they landed in Sierra Leone (West Africa). That is where they started their journey and became great businessmen and diamond dealers, a continuing business my uncles still run in Antwerp, Zaire and South Africa.

Among the food and ingredients they enjoyed in Africa was Peeya (avocados), a fruit they brought back to their homeland whenever they visited. Pineapples and mangoes, fish and prawns and peanuts and palm oil were other kinds of African food that was enjoyed and some families incorporated some Middle Eastern influence in the cooking of them, as in this recipe.

Other people who migrated to Brazil and Argentina, introduced avocados with honey and as a milkshake; actually this is one of the most regarded and highly demanded item at many juice shops and restaurants.

All in all, as much as I am known for my sweet tooth, I still prefer avocado with Middle Eastern flavours.

Ingredients

3 ripe Hass avocados

5 sprigs of spring onions

½ bunch fresh parsley

Handful of fresh mint leaves

Juice of a lime

Sprinkle of cayenne pepper (quarter of a teaspoon or whatever is your limit)

Drizzle of extra virgin olive oil

Method

1) Wash the fresh vegetables thoroughly and chop semi fine, cut the avocados in half, de-seed and peel. Cut the avocados length way and place in a semi deep bowl.

2) Add the freshly chopped vegetables and the juice of a lemon with olive oil, season with salt and cayenne pepper.

Fatet Batinjan

This fatte is composed of fried aubergines, minced lamb and tomato sauce, all covered with yoghurt and tahini sauce and topped by pine nuts.

Ingredients

6 baby aubergines, washed, peeled and salted

1 toasted pitta bread, cooked in the oven until crisp then crushed randomly to medium sized pieces

4 cloves garlic, crushed

500g natural yoghurt

100g tahini or sesame sauce

200g minced lamb

3 tbsp tomato paste

100g pine nuts

100g unsalted butter

1 tsp ground cinnamon

Salt to season

Dash of black pepper

Sprinkle of paprika to garnish

Method

1) Whack the pitta bread in the oven until golden crisp at 180 °C for about 10 minutes, then break into medium pieces after it has cooled down.

2) Peel the baby aubergines and deep-fry until golden, then set aside on kitchen towel to drain any excess oil.

3) In a hot pan, sizzle some oil and cook the minced lamb with some seasoning according to taste: salt, black pepper and a touch of ground cinnamon if you wish. Add the tomato paste and cook evenly for about 10 minutes on very low heat.

4) In a bowl pour the natural yoghurt and tahini, whisk together very well for a semi thick consistency, add 3 cloves of crushed garlic and season well with salt.

To assemble the Fate

1) Grab your favourite semi-deep dish, rub its centre with crushed garlic and layer the toasted bread.

2) Top up the bread with a layer of the minced lamb and tomato (half the quantity) and then layer the aubergines; you can cut the aubergines in half or leave them whole.

3) Add the remaining layer of minced lamb and then top up with the yoghurt and tahini mix.

4) Into a hot pan melt the 100g butter and toast the pine nuts until golden; now pour everything on top of the yoghurt while it's sizzling.

'Ahha! Now that is a taste from Heaven to Earth. The best way to eat fatte is immediately while the butter is sizzling on the yoghurt: the combination of the deeply toasted nuts with the fresh cold yoghurt is indescribable. That on its own is enough reason for you try to discover your Lebanese taste buds.

I remember my aunts gathering the whole family on a Sunday brunch for a Fatte Feast (she made two types of fatte, one with chickpeas and the other with lamb tongues). They usually wait till April when the weather is milder and everyone gathers to experience the contrast of hot chickpeas or lamb tongues with the cold yoghurt and tahini mix, topped by toasted pine nuts and sizzling butter or ghee.'

Fatet Humus

Fatte is often enjoyed as a breakfast on the weekends when family and friends gather. The chickpea fatte is the simplest of all, but it does go harder in levels; I believe it is not unusual for the Lebanese to unlock different levels of flavours and ingredients mixed together and you know what, it's just amazing.

Fatet Humus is usually bought from the *Fawal*. This is a local shop selling cooked breakfast to the community; it also sells *foul* which is fava beans and chickpeas with garlic, lemon juice and olive oil, as well as fatte with tongues, lamb cubes and lamb legs. The list is endless.

The word *fattee* (also written *fatte*, *fett* or *fatet*) means 'scattered' in Arabic: in other words, one scatters something soft on the plate. I would imagine in this case it refers to scattering the toasted bread on the yoghurt. It is a popular term, used in the term '*Fett khobez*' which means to scatter bread, and ironically in '*Fett masari*' (scatter money) when someone is poor.

I believe that origianal people scattered bread and chickpeas in the bowl then added some yoghurt to give the dish a bit of character to it. Then some ghee and nuts again were scattered on top. However, this dish has evolved incredibly through the ages: nowadays one can enjoy fatte with aubergines, or lamb tongues or lamb legs.

Ingredients

500g boiled, ready-to-eat chickpeas
2 pitta bread, toasted until crisp and dry
1kg natural yoghurt
5 cloves crushed garlic with a hint of salt
30 ml tahini or sesame sauce (this is optional)
Salt to taste (in the yoghurt)
150g butter or ghee
Handful of pine nuts
Sprinkle of ground paprika (for garnish)

Tip: You can use directly from the can or soak the chickpeas the night before. Next day bring to boil with a teaspoon of bicarbonate of soda. This usually takes about two and a half hours until the chickpeas are thoroughly cooked. My mother uses fresh chickpeas: when thoroughly cooked and cooled she takes off their outer layer and packs them into parcels, ready to freeze.

Method

1) Whack the pitta bread into the oven at 180 °C and let it dry out and become golden crisp (this should take about 10 minutes in the oven). Once cooled, break into squares and leave on the side.

2) Pour the natural yoghurt into a bowl and add the tahini with two splashes of cold water.

3) Add the crushed garlic into the yoghurt mixture, saving a little bit for later, and whisk until well combined.

4) Season with salt according to taste – you may wish to add more water to the yoghurt mix depending on the texture and quality of the tahini. I find the yoghurt mix delicious at a medium thick consistency.

5) Rub the remaining crushed garlic into the serving bowl, add the broken pitta bread and spread all over as a layer.

6) Add a layer of the cooked chickpeas and spread all over. It's okay to include some of the liquid from the boiled chickpeas as this enhances the flavour and soaks into the pitta bread underneath. If using chickpeas from the can then just heat in a pan with some water.

7) Toast the pine nuts in a frying pan for a minute and then add the butter and let it melt and sizzle.

8) Now pour over the yoghurt in the dish, scatter more toasted pitta bread on top and a sprinkle of paprika, and there you go! Top with the sizzling butter and pine nuts to enjoy the greatest and simplest flavours embedded in one dish.

Humus Bil Lahme

The original name of the dish is Humus Bil Kawarma: *'Kawarma'* is when minced lamb or mini-diced lamb cubes are cooked with a higher quantity of pure fat. It is cooked until reduced with extra salt and then stored in airtight jars for the winter season. This is one of the popular methods of preserving lamb cubes for the winter season and is used as combination with many different dishes such as fried eggs, humus and *kishk* (fermented milk mixed with crushed wheat).

Kawarma is a difficult process and not many people have the skills nowadays, let alone that it is a heavy food. It is commonly used in the mountains of Lebanon and most of all the eastern region of Baalbeck and the Bekaa. The villages are too far from the city and suburbs, which explains why people are in need of such a preservation method. I still remember very well when our neighbours who came from Baalbeck used to give us a jar of Kawarma; in return, of course, my grandmother gave them pomegranate syrup and also mulberry and rose syrup. This is always the habit of the Lebanese after the summer holidays when most of them return to the city from their home villages with yearly stock for the whole year such as zaatar mix, cumin mix, crushed wheat (fine or coarse), fruit syrups, jams and conserves and all kinds of pickles and tomato puree.

Ingredients

Humus or chickpeas puree (see page 64 for method)
200g lamb fillets diced carefully into small pieces
50g pine nuts for garnish
Ground paprika for garnish

Method

1) This could be the humus you buy from a quality store or it could be the one you do at home.

2) The most important of this recipe is the taste of the lamb and its combination with the humus.

3) Into a hot pan, add a drizzle of vegetable oil and the lamb cubes. Toss for about 8 minutes or until cooked, season with salt and add the pine nuts to be toasted with them.

4) Spread the humus in your desired plate and scatter the lamb cubes and pine nuts on top. Garnish with some finely chopped parsley and ground paprika.

Makali

This is a traditional medley of aubergines, cauliflower and courgettes all sliced and deep-fried. It may feel that these vegetables are flavourless but there is so much one can do with them: some eat them with traditional garlic and lemon juice, others opt for yoghurt, cucumber, dry mint and garlic salad. However there are many other twists, as shown as the picture below. In addition to the yoghurt mix I also made parsley and sweet red pepper sauce with lemon juice and salt.

Lemon and Garlic Sauce

Ingredients

3 cloves of garlic

Squeezed juice of a lemon

Pinch of salt

Method

1) Crush the garlic with a pinch of salt.

2) Mix together and serve with the fried vegetables.

Parsley with red pepper or chilli

Ingredients

Parsley

Red pepper

Chilli (optional)

Juice of 2 lemons

Salt

Method

1) Finely chop the parsley, red pepper and chilli (if used).

2) Add the lemon juice.

3) Season with salt and mix.

Moghrabiye and Pomegranate

This is a starter combining durum wheat pearls with pomegranate rubies. In my recipes I often enjoy going the extra mile; although I have shared the original recipe (page 131), I still wanted to give my readers a '3D vision' into other possibilities! This will no doubt enhance their appreciation of different approaches to home cooking.

My aunt passed this recipe to me last summer, when we were on holidays in Beirut. I was shocked it existed but she explained:

> **'Dear darling, when I was in France it was popular in restaurants to serve a variety of couscous salad, some with red pepper and others with fresh herbs and tomato sauce. When I came back to Beirut, I recreated the same with moghrabiye which is really tasteless and requires many strong flavours to enhance it.'**

Experimenting with the recipe, you may want to toss the moghrabiye pearls with 50g of butter and then pour into the assembling bowl, dress it up and then serve.

Ingredients

200g dried beads of moghrabiye (found in many Middle Eastern shops, such as on Edgware Road in London)
100g pomegranate (sweet and sour)
4 sprigs of spring onions, finely chopped
Couple sprigs of fresh parsley, roughly chopped

Dressing

Juice of 1 lemon
Juice of 1 lime
Juice of ½ tangerine
1 tsp ground caraway
1 tsp ground cumin
Dash of black pepper
Salt to taste
30ml extra virgin olive oil

Method

1) Add the moghrabiye pearls to hot boiling water and let them cook for 15 minutes (*al dente*) or 25 minutes (thoroughly cooked).

2) Pour into a semi-flat sieve and allow to cool. Add a drizzle of olive oil to prevent from the pearls from sticking together while cooling down.

3) In the meantime, wash the herbs thoroughly and chop finely, extract the citrus juices and whisk up the dressing separately on the side.

4) Cut the pomegranate in the middle, and empty those rare red rubies onto a plate.

5) You can now start assembling this extravaganza: empty the pearls into a deep bowl, add the chopped herbs, dressing, mix slightly.

6) Pour into your desired dish or service plate, sprinkle as many 'red rubies' (pomegranate seeds) as possible and share with your loved and dear ones.

MEZZE

M EZZE ARE EXTENSIVE and could lead to a never-ending book. Lebanon is very rich in the use of ingredients and different flavours together and the variety of mezze is the result of everyday trial and error.

In this modest book of the Lebanese cuisine, I intended to use a limited number of mezzes and some I combined with the salads too. This is because many of the other mezzes are originally bought from special sandwich shops. Falafels tend not to be made and eaten at home: why bother when there are several excellent shops around the local village, or even on local streets of Beirut?

The shops are amazing, the smell and the theatrical presentation is extremely seductive. After all, despite all the surrounding negative factors the Lebanese still honour their ancestors' attitude to food and take pride in it.

The Falafel Shop

*A man preparing falafels for service, at **Basta Tahta** in Beirut. One of the best falafels I've tasted in the city.*

Preparing the sandwiches with a variety of pickles and fresh vegetables, sesame sauce and chilli if you prefer.

According to the Lebanese, the way to have the perfect gastro-nomic experience with falafel is to visit your favourite shop amidst the chaos and ask for your favourite choice of variety vegetables that comes with the falafel. The experience is amazing and much nicer at home than with the artificial and commercial ones here in Europe. (Falafel as a recipe will be discussed in detail in another forthcoming project).

The Shawarma Shop

In my days 'Barbar' was the reputable shawarma shop and the sandwiches were renowned for their deliciousness and balanced ingredients. Both my aunts and my uncle would to head to the famous shopping street known as 'El Hamra'; we bought lamb or chicken shawarma with extra pickles and tarator (sesame sauce) and then head to 'Malik El Batata' – known as the 'King of Chips' – and he would serve the fried chips in little white cartons topped with ketchup and some wooden sticks. Oh my God, my favourite thing as a child was to enjoy this white carton on my own.

Dips and Tips

Over the past 10 years, dips are becoming increasingly popular and widely available at supermarket shelves and as starters in many contemporary restaurants.

I must admit, they are usually very easy to prepare and it is fun to gather friends and family over to share the unique taste of each ingredient and its mix.

In my home, sharing dips bring us all together on the sofa while watching TV and it is certainly a warm gesture on your dining table when guests are waiting for the main dish and yourself to sit with them.

Humus

500g chickpeas, boiled
4 cloves peeled garlic
Juice of 2 lemons
150g tahini sauce
Salt to taste
Sprinkle of ground paprika

Beetroot

2 cooked beetroots, mashed
3 tbsp humus puree
½ tsp balsamic vinegar
Salt to taste
Sprinkle of sesame and toasted pine nuts

Avocado Puree

2 ripe Haas avocados, mashed

Juice of 1 lemon

2 cloves of garlic, peeled and crushed

Salt to taste

Sprinkle of ground cayenne pepper

Method (for all dips)

1) Puree in a food blender and empty into your favourite dip bowls or straight onto mini crispy toast.

Baba Ganouj

The direct meaning of Baba Ganouj is 'the spoiled father'. He must have been a vicar who practised great influence on the locals and loved eating aubergines with garlic and tahini! Aubergine is widely eaten all over the Middle East. It used to be known as the 'vegetable of the kings'; only the Sultans were allowed to eat it in Turkey.

'I remember when I used to return from school and find my grandfather and uncles waiting at the dining table, chatting and drinking arack while my grandmother and aunt Samia were preparing fried sardines and deep-fried pitta bread – Mmmm, the latter were deliciously crispy. One nostalgic image stuck in my memory is of a deep white bowl with a picture of a little lady in pink; my aunt in her white robe pounded the grilled aubergines into the bowl until semi-pureed then asked me to pour the tahini and lemon juice. She carried on pounding and tasting until she adjusted the balance of salt and lemon with the tahini; she spread it into an oval platter and scattered over the pomegranate and finely chopped parsley.'

I hated sardines; I guess as a 7 year-old I was put off by the whole look of it. However, I enjoyed the deep-fried bread with the baba ganouj and of course some Pepsi instead of arack.

The contradictory tastes of sweet and sour pomegranate combined with strong nutty flavours of the tahini just explodes onto your palette.

Those were the days – when the Lebanese celebrated their cuisine three times per day, people could travel from one town to another, enjoy different flavours at different regions. I am just waiting to relive this feeling again with my fellow Lebanese.

'I hope we are not waiting for another independence day, surviving the irritations of the whole Middle Eastern regions. We are Lebanese people: we love life, we love to live, eat, drink and be merry.'

Ingredients

2 large aubergines
4 cloves of garlic
Juice of 2 lemons
30 ml extra virgin olive oil
100g tahini sauce
2 tbsp strained yoghurt
Handful of sour pomegranate

Method

1) Wash the aubergines thoroughly, wrap them with silver foil and fork all around it, allowing a direct flame to go through.

2) Place the aubergines on a direct fire on the hub and keep turning around every 3 minutes, for a total of about 15 minutes each (depending on the size of the aubergines).

3) In the meantime, peel the garlic and crush, squeeze the lemon juice and mix them with the tahini and the yoghurt.

4) Take the aubergines off the heat and allow to cool. Peel off the skin and chop them finely, in any way you choose. It is also quicker to put in a food processor and give it couple of clicks as you don't want it thoroughly pureed.

5) Now add the semi-pureed or chopped aubergines into the tahini bowl and mix thoroughly until all combined, add salt to taste.

6) Spread in a platter or semi-deep bowl. Garnish with pomegranate and some finely chopped parsley and a drizzle of extra virgin olive oil.

Labne Motawame

Labne is strained yoghurt. It is very thick in texture, but creamy and delicious. It is one of those spreads one has at any time; it is very popular eaten with olives and baby cucumbers. On the other hand, many restaurants have developed the taste of Labne a little bit further; some have added garlic and others fragrant dry mint. I love both flavours and sometimes fancy combining them together: after all, garlic and mint form a great marriage.

I remember visiting my paternal grandparents' village in Sultanieh in the southern region of the Lebanon. The village is about 650m above sea level so it's pretty cold in the winter.

The only heating we had was a medium-sized chimney running on twigs; it was placed in the middle of the living room and we all gathered around it on the carpeted floor. My grandmother would prepare platters of labne, cheese spreads, zaatar (thyme mix) and we would heat the pitta bread on the chimney until it was semi crisp and dip into the labne and zaatar. Oh my God; that was unbelievable. The simple setting, the taste, the experience of gentle heat and dipping some home-prepared olives into your favourite platter was just pretty irresistible. I still remember every moment and it's just amazing how time flies; but a good food experience is definitely embedded into our senses and above all into our subconscious mind.

Ingredients

6 tbsp strained yoghurt
1 clove of garlic, crushed
Sprinkle of salt to taste
Sprinkle of dry mint
Drizzle of extra virgin olive oil

Method

1) Whisk the ingredients all together and spread in a mini plate.

Note: The best way to enjoy this is with Arabic bread, olives and a cup of tea. On the other hand, people also enjoy this combination as part of the extended mezze, especially through the spring and summer seasons. Labne or strained yoghurt is cold, soft and smooth and it refreshes the pallet amidst all the other strong and flavoured mezze. In some regions of the Lebanon, garlic and mint flavoured labne are often used as a stuffing in kibbe.

'I recently ate in a restaurant in Jezzine, a beautiful village in the south of Lebanon. Jezzine is famous for its scenery; you can enjoy the high mountains, all beautifully green, fresh springs and waterfalls as cold as ice even throughout its hottest summers.

We ordered a good sized mezze but the attraction on the menu was a house special kibbe. It was a chargrilled kibbe stuffed with garlic and mint labne. I immediately gave in to this temptation: the combination of the dry burghul and beef alongside a fresh and yoghurt texture was beyond description. My dazzled senses wondered how rich the Lebanese mezze could be, let alone the whole cuisine itself, and how much culture is embedded into this tiny country on the map of the world.'

Batata Hara (Spicy Potato)

Ingredients

500g potatoes, peeled and diced

1 bunch of fresh coriander, thoroughly washed and roughly chopped

5 cloves of garlic, peeled and crushed

Salt to taste

1 tsp ground paprika

1 red chilli chopped (optional)

500ml vegetable oil (for deep-frying)

Method

1) Deep-fry the diced potatoes until they are a light golden colour, then leave on kitchen towel to drain excess oil.

2) Wash the roughly chopped coriander and add a drizzle of oil to a pan.

3) Stir-fry the coriander, crushed garlic and chopped chilli.

4) Add the potatoes and stir fry gently on low heat. Add salt to taste, add the ground paprika and place in a dish.

5) Please, please add a squeeze of lemon juice!

Sluluk Bil Zeyt (Stuffed Swiss Chard)

Stuffed Swiss chard is one of the most tantalizing dishes of all time! The combination of the fresh vegetables cooked in lemon juice and virgin olive oil creates an impeccable taste.

Stuffing vegetables and vine leaves is native to all the countries in the Middle East, yet each incorporates their own special touch. In Persia, for example, saffron is added to the stuffing; the Turkish, Greeks and Cypriots cook the stuffing and then roll it in vine leaves. However, each method possess a different mouthwatering experience that each one of us can try; it is definitely not about competition and who can make the stuffing the most authentic.

Stuffed Swiss chard is a common dish to Beirut; outside the capital city, locals are famous for the dish and it is commonly made in the winter. Swiss chard is cheaper than vine leaves and widely available throughout winter in the city. On the other hand, vine leaves are not available in the city and are more of a village plantation; that is why this dish is similarly to ones using vine leaves.

My grandmother would always pick plenty of vine leaves in the summer time and store them in jars to last throughout winter. A lot of city residents also buy such jars from various villages or receive them as presents from family members or friends.

Ingredients

4 bunches Swiss chard

3 medium sized potatoes

4 large carrots

2 vine tomatoes

3 onions

Juice of 3 lemons

100ml extra virgin olive oil

1 tsp pomegranate molasses (optional)

Hint of chilli powder (optional)

Salt to taste (often about 2 tsp)

Water to cover for simmering

The Stuffing Ingredients

1 bunch of parsley, finely chopped

2 bunches spring onions, finely chopped

10 mint leaves, finely chopped

4 large ripe vine tomatoes

100g rice

Juice of a lemon

Drizzle of olive oil

Salt to taste

1 tbsp pomegranate molasses (optional, but it
  definitely enhances and deepens the flavour)

Hint of chilli powder (optional)

Method

1) Assemble the premium layers of the Suluk pot: sliced potatoes, sliced onions, carrots and vine tomatoes. These enhance the flavours, especially when the food is left to rest and cool in the pot for 24 hours before service.

2) Wash all the vegetables thoroughly and chop the ones for the stuffing finely and mix them with rice in a bowl, seasoning with lemon, salt and olive oil. Slice the other vegetables such as carrots, potatoes, onions and tomatoes and place them in the cooking pot as shown in the picture below.

3) Wash the Swiss chard thoroughly and cut off the stem. Blanch in boiling water for 15 seconds and remove into a sieve. This is a very delicate procedure so please deal with the chard leaves with care and love!

4) Sieve the rice and vegetable stuffing and save the juice for cooking later as a stock. On a board, place the chard and put one teaspoon

of the stuffing in the middle and roll like a cigar: see the picture below.

5)   Place 'cigars' in the pot as shown opposite and build it up to the top. Cover with the rest of the stock and add some more stock and water to cover.

6)   Place a heavy, heat-resistant plate or round bowl to apply pressure to the cigars and bring to boil.

7)   Once it reaches boiling point, reduce the heat to the lowest and allow a cooking time for an hour or until the rice is cooked – you can check this with a fork.

Stuffed Swiss chard ready to eat!

Batinjan Bil Zeyt

This is a popular dish, usually combined with vine leaves. It is exactly the same as the Swiss chard recipe above (Sluluk Bil Zeyt). Instead of using chard, core the baby aubergines and clean them thoroughly. For the vegetables and rice stuffing, apply exactly the same amounts and steps as in the Sluluk Bil Zeyt recipe. However, this needs about an hour's worth of cooking on low heat after it reaches boiling point, or until the aubergines are thoroughly cooked.

Kibbe

Kibbe is one of the top-notch Lebanese national dishes; whenever people talk about Lebanese food kibbe and tabbouleh come immediately to the mind or memories of the speaker.

Despite the rich variety of the Lebanese cuisine, both kibbe and tabbouleh are the outstanding examples of this small country's finest foods. The Turkish, Greeks, Syrians and other neighbouring countries have served these dishes over centuries, yet the Lebanese have proven their mastery of the art both of constructing the kibbe and of balancing its fragrant flavours.

I suppose the other countries in the region enjoy kibbe and various methods of cooking it. However, the Lebanese as usual have carried this the extra mile; obviously our Phoenician ancestors were adventurous, while the Assyrians who resided in our mountains were always happy to try food!

My grandmother would always pound the beef topside on a marbled stone with a wooden pestle.

Ingredients

500g defatted topside of beef

250g fine brown burghul (crushed wheat)

2 onions, chopped in half

¼ bunch of fresh mint

½ red pepper, torn into two pieces

1 green or red chilli (depending on your taste)

150g cumin/kibbe mix

Salt to taste

Note: You may find sachets of the cumin/ kibbe mix in Middle Eastern shops; alternatively, just mix some ground cumin with a teaspoon of allspice and a teaspoon of black pepper. Also, ask the butcher to mince the topside of the beef: this will mean a less chaotic process at home.

Method

1) Soak the crushed wheat with a handful of water for 10 minutes before use.

2) Mix the minced beef with the crushed wheat and put into a meat grinder. Add the onions, red pepper and mint.

3) Mix all together, then mince one more time until all flavours are thoroughly combined.

4) Season with salt and the cumin mix and allow to rest.

Stuffing

450g minced lamb

200g finely chopped onions

100g pine kernels

50g pomegranate molasses or a ½ tsp of sumac

1 tsp ground cinnamon

Salt to taste

40ml vegetable oil

Method

1) Add the vegetable oil to a hot pan and sweat the onions, seasoning with a dash of salt.

2) Add the minced lamb and pine kernels. Stir from time to time until lamb is thoroughly cooked (i.e. when the meat becomes brown).

3) Reduce the heat, season with pomegranate molasses, cinnamon and salt to taste. Give it another stir and then remove from heat.

4) Empty the stuffing into a colander or sieve and leave until thoroughly cooled and drained of excess fluids and oil.

5) In the meantime, prepare the kibbe mix into equal-sized ping pong ball shapes.

6) Make a hole in the ball and start digging deeper, until the rounded kibbe walls are thinner and the hole is larger. Put a teaspoon of the stuffing into the hold and close the topside of the kibbe.

7) The kibbe can then be frozen for later use or deep-fried immediately in vegetable oil.

Note: To aid stuffing process, keep a bowl containing cold water and some vegetable oil by your side. Every time your hands get sticky, soak in the bowl and use the liquid on the kibbe to make it smoother and easier to handle.

'Celebrating the summer holidays in Jbaa (Southern Lebanon), my grandmother's village: my grandfather went to the local butcher as soon as the summer dew was on the car (I am talking about 4.30 or 5 o'clock in the morning). He bought fresh raw liver with some leeyeh (fat from the sheep's tail): this would be eaten in small cubes with the raw liver, while some was kept for later to be used with the kibbe to make it more velvety.

My grandmother sat on a cushion on the floor and started by adding a dash of salt to the beef to pound it; the topside becomes pinker as it is hand-pureed. A pink, full-blossomed virgin beef appears on the blataa (marbled stone) – blooming with colour, flavour and fragrance. I remember her asking me to pick a handful of fresh basil and mint leaves from the pots on the balcony. She then pounded these herbs with the cumin mix, salt and a hint of chilli; I enjoyed sitting beside her as she used to give me some of the pureed pink beef in a bread and – aahhh – nothing in the world beats that feeling of a combined cultural, traditional and folkloric food experience. That is the ultimate umami experience: it isn't about bizarre foods or scooping fresh monkey brains in Thailand, nor about experiencing crocodile meat and chips. It is all about sharing the preparation of the dish with the people you most love and enjoying the full-on flavour in your own way.'

Kibbe with a minty yoghurt at a restaurant in Jezzine, a southern village of Lebanon.

Frake

Frake is similar to raw kibbe yet it has more beef than fine burghul in it. It is a highly nutritious dish and full of flavour, and everyone in Lebanon gathers around the family table on the weekend to have the best frake ever.

Each kibbe or frake will only taste as good as the mixture of Kamoune (cumin) mix used on it (see page 89). As mentioned earlier, this mix differs slightly from one region to another; for example the southern region locals add dry roses and dry chilli peppers, while the locals of the mountains of Lebanon just add the cloves, cumin, black and red peppercorns. It can also be used with tomato, potato and lentils.

Ingredients

500g topside of beef, pureed in a food processor

150g fine burghul or crushed wheat

100g cumin mix

¼ bunch fresh mint leaves

1 large onion

Couple of chillies (optional)

½ sweet red pepper

Salt to taste

30 ml extra virgin olive oil

Selection of crispy vegetables: radish, spring onions, sweet white onions, fresh mint leaves, tomatoes

Method

1) To help to puree the topside of the beef, ask the butcher to debone it and dice it to medium-sized pieces.

2) Place into your food processor with a dash of salt until it's pink and pureed. Try to remove any white fibrous tissues in order to make the paste more velvety; these can be easily spotted during the puree process.

3) Once the beef is pureed, store in the refrigerator until you have finished the next step.

4) Soak the fine burghul with some water and a dash of extra virgin olive oil and leave on the side.

5) Create the Kamoune mix (see page 89).

6) Mix the Kamoune mix with the burghul and lay on the side of the pureed beef and that is ready to go as it is or even make it to frake.

7) You may serve this as seen in the above picture, flatten some of the beef puree and enjoy with the cumin mix and fresh vegetables and a drizzle of extra virgin olive oil.

8) On the other hand to make frake, dip your fine hands into the beef puree and apply some extra virgin olive oil, salt to taste and some cumin mix. The ratio here is personal, however the tradition is to have more beef then burghul and just make it like a ball and then press it in the palm of your hands. Place in your favourite flat platter, drizzle with extra virgin olive oil and enjoy eating this famous mezze with your hands.

Hint: Be aware that the beef has to be fresh and your butcher is that of a reputable and trusted one because this recipe is to be consumed raw otherwise please make as kibbe burgers and deep-fry.

The Kamoune Mix

Ingredients

Onions

Fresh mint leaves

Fine crushed wheat (preferably white), soaked

Fresh Greek basil leaves

Red chillies (optional)

Traditional Cumin mix: cumin seeds, black, green and
red peppercorns, cloves, dry roses, dry chilli, cinnamon

Method

1) Add the onions, fresh mint, red pepper and the cumin mix into the food processor and blitz.

2) Add salt to taste and as much chilli as you desire.

Sambousek Bil Lahme

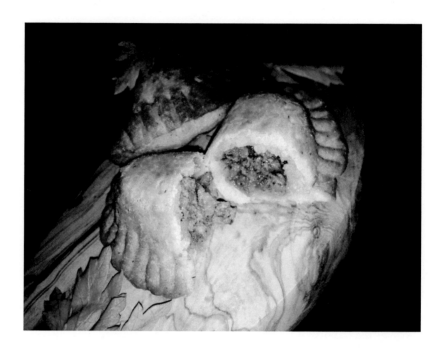

Ingredients

2 cups of all-purpose flour and pinch of salt

100g soft butter

1 tbsp baking powder

1 free range egg

Stuffing recipe (see Kibbe balls, page 83)

Tip: If you find it hard to knead, add about a handful of lukewarm water.

Method

1) In a bowl add the flour sieved through with a pinch of salt.

2) Add the butter and start working it with your hands until the mixture is bound all together.

3) Add the baking powder and egg, knead the dough until all formed together. At this stage you may need to add a touch of water and you may not so I leave it to your judgement; if the dough is too stiff then add a dash of luke warm tap water otherwise allow to rest in a warm place for about 30 minutes.

My prince is enjoying his sambousek. I must admit, as a mother of two the kids enjoyed these activities with me on rainy days or even when my husband was away on work.

There is also the cheese version and here it is.

Ingredients

200g halloumi cheese, grated
100g strained yoghurt
1 tbsp poppy seeds or 1 tbsp dry mint
Salt to taste

Method

1) Mix all ingredients until they are bound together.

2) Free up your working top and dust this and your rolling pin with some flour.

3) Roll the dough as flat as possible. Using your favourable pastry-cutter ring size, cut through the dough to make circular shapes to be used as pouches for the meat or cheese stuffing.

4) Place a teaspoon of the stuffing into each of the cut circles and then flip one side on to the other.

5) Attach them together firmly with your fingers and then cover your fork with some flour and fork the pastry all around the sides so it can stick firmly.

6) At this stage you can either freeze them or deep-fry them in vegetable oil.

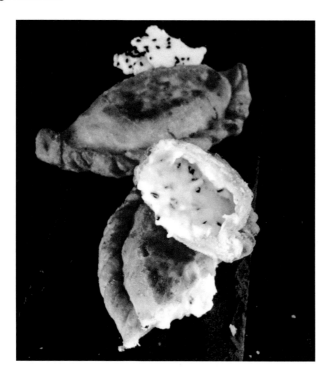

Note: if you are going to freeze these, please lay them first into flat trays until they are hard frozen, then move them into bags of a dozen each. You can keep them frozen for three months.

Lahme Bil Ajeen

Lahme bil Ajeen, or Sfeeha, is a flat dough topped with minced lamb or beef, mixed with finely chopped onions, tomatoes and Lebanon's seven spice mix (cumin, paprika, coriander, nutmeg, cloves, cinnamon and black pepper). It is one of the most popular snacks. The flat dough comes in several sizes ranging from large to small; others come smaller with squared corners known as Sfeeha Baalbakieh. The 'Sun City' (Baalbeck in eastern Lebanon), a popular tourist site and the site of Lebanon's Roman ruins, is famous for the best Lahme Bil Ajeen/Sfeeha.

According to *Food in Antiquity*, both the Romans and Egyptians were famous for kneading dough and making large oval flat breads; funnily enough, both these civilisations invaded the Lebanon and settled for long periods. Working with flat dough is always creative and when it comes to experimenting the flavour combinations of food and spices, the sky is the limit.

On the other hand, I believe it acquired its alternative name of *Sfeeha* from the Egyptian word '*Safayeh*', meaning a group of opened containers. One may argue the truth of this naïve observation; however, relying just on my memory I have seen the group of flat doughs on a conveyor given to customers who would fill them with their choice of toppings.

I remember that my aunt used to send me to the local bakery with the mince mix every weekend, at about midday. The guy would give me six wooden tops, each with six flat doughs; I would have to top it with my mix and then he would bake them in his wooden oven. I can never forget the hot sensation and fresh smell of the baked mince and spices: it was just heavenly. Sfeeha is very popular on lazy summer days, and always enjoyed with fresh yoghurt drink.

All in all, it just tastes delicious and the smaller ones are even more scrumptious. Please give it a try! Not only would your guests love it but family members will also try to snatch them before the guests arrive.

Ingredients for the Dough

4 cups all purpose flour

10g instant yeast

¾ cup vegetable oil

Sprinkle of salt

1 cup of lukewarm water

Ingredients or the Mince Mix

750g minced lamb or beef (optional)

4 beef tomatoes, finely chopped

3 onions, finely chopped

Salt to taste

1 tsp pomegranate molasses

2 chillies finely chopped (optional)

1 tsp seven spices

Method

1) Knead all the dough ingredients together and allow to rest for about two hours in a warm place.

2) Dust your work top and the rolling pin with some flour.

3) Grab a piece of the dough and shape it into a sphere about the size of a tennis ball. Flatten the dough with your rolling pin until reasonably flat.

4) Apply the minced lamb mix all around the flat dough and twirl the dough slightly all around the sides to give it an edge.

5) Add just a little dash of vegetable oil into a baking tray, place the lahme bil ajeen and bake in the oven for about 10-12 minutes on 180°C or until the meat is thoroughly cooked and the dough is golden in colour.

FAMILY MEALS

T HERE ARE PLENTY of family meals and mostly are vegetables or beans stews with tender lamb cubes or chicken. I chose
the most popular; most are not included in the Lebanese cookery
books I have read in Europe.

Riz Ala Djaj

This is usually boiled baby chicken (also known as a poussin) served with rice and cooked with minced lamb, nuts and five spices. Riz ala djaj is very traditional and extremely popular: the meat is sometimes substituted with large lamb cubes or even a slow-cooked lamb shoulder.

I remember the way my grandmother made this dish: she would boil the chicken and its aromatics to make a stock which is used to cook the rice. Whatever is left is served as a broth alongside the chicken and the rice. However, some people have twisted this recipe a little and they have found it easier to marinate the chicken and then roast it in the oven. This is because they prefer the chicken crispy or they believe it creates more flavour because it retains some of its juices.

Ingredients

350g minced lamb
1 baby chicken/poussin
1 mug of rice
2 mugs of hot boiling chicken stock
50g pine kernels (optional)
50g pistachios (optional)
50g almonds (optional)
1 tsp salt or to taste
2 tsp ground cinnamon

Note: cooking the chicken needs a couple of cardamoms, cinnamon stick, any stock cube, carrot, celery stalk, onion, and some cloves and black pepper, salt to taste.

Method

1) Wash the baby chicken under cold water with some salt and lemon; bring it to boil and add all the aromatics as this will enhance the flavour of the stock and will be used in cooking the rice.

2) Drizzle some vegetable oil in a pot with a knob of butter. Add the pine kernels, pistachios and almonds (if used) and cook until golden. Add the minced lamb and stir until thoroughly cooked and stir gently.

3) Add the mug of rice and stir gently, season with some salt and cinnamon and add two mugs of the boiling chicken stock. Reduce the heat to the lowest gas mark and let it simmer for about 15 minutes or until the rice is thoroughly cooked.

4) Traditionally the rice is served in an oval dish with scattered chicken pieces and nuts all over the top; however, this time I decided to twist my service time a little bit. I cut the boiled chicken on the board into four pieces and sealed it in a hot pan with a knob of butter; then served it with rice and nuts and some yoghurt or salad, or just the chicken broth.

Sabanekh Wa Ruz

Ingredients

1kg fresh spinach

350g minced lamb

100g pine nuts

6 cloves garlic, peeled and crushed

½ bunch fresh coriander

2 knobs of butter (one for the garlic and coriander, the other is for the minced lamb and pine nuts)

Juice of 2 lemons

Salt to taste

Method

1) Wash the fresh spinach thoroughly; and add to a pot of boiling water, sprinkle a bit of salt and a squeeze of lemon. Bring to the boil again.

2) In the meantime, peel the garlic cloves and crush them with a pestle and mortar. Wash the coriander thoroughly, chop roughly and set aside in a sieve to remove excess water.

3) Melt a knob of butter in a frying pan, add the minced lamb and the pine nuts and cook thoroughly. Season with salt to taste and a tip of a teaspoon of ground cinnamon; cook until the pine nuts are golden.

4) Add the minced lamb mix into the spinach pot and let it cook on medium heat. Once it starts boiling reduce heat to minimum.

5) In a frying pan, add a knob of butter and toss the crushed garlic and coriander for 3 minutes or so, then flip into the spinach pot.

6) Add the juice of lemon, season with salt to taste and allow to simmer on minimum heat for about 35 -40 minutes.

7) Serve with pilau rice and a couple of wedges of lemon and some chilli if desirable.

How to make pilau rice

1) Boil water in the kettle.

2) Put a handful of vermicelli into a hot pan, drizzled with some vegetable oil and a knob of butter.

3) Stir gently until the vermicelli is golden.

4) Add 1 mug of basmati rice; season with salt and stir slowly.

5) Measure two mugs of hot boiling water and add to the rice.

6) Cover and simmer for 15 minutes on very low heat.

Sayadieh

This word actually means 'the fisherman's net'.People cook the sayadieh in many different ways: some add turmeric and saffron to give it the yellow colour and others just add the fish spices such as cumin, cloves and black pepper. Some people add onions and others combine the onions with prawns and sultanas. All in all there is not a definite or fixed recipe and probably the reason it is called 'the fisherman's net' is because you can cook it with whatever you may find in the 'net'.

Ingredients

1kg cod fillets or sea bass

4 tbsp olive oil to massage the fish fillets

4 large Spanish onions

1 mug of rice

2 tsp Sayadie or fish spices

2 tsp salt or according to taste

50g pine kernels

50g almonds

40ml vegetable oil to sweat onions and prepare the dish

Note: Fish spices are available in many Middle Eastern shops. If this was out of reach then you add 1 teaspoon of turmeric, a couple of saffron threads, 1 teaspoon of ground cumin, ½ teaspoon of black pepper, ½ teaspoon of ground cinnamon, ½ teaspoon of ground cardamom, a couple of clover and 1 teaspoon of ground coriander.

Method

1) Season the fillet of cod on both sides with salt and olive oil, put in the oven for about 8 minutes.

2) In the meantime, slice the onions into trenches and put into a hot pan, sweat them until they are golden crisp but please keep this pot as you will use it again).

3) Move the golden onions and add them to the boiling fish stock; this will enhance the entire stock flavour and darken its colour.

4) In the pot where you sweated the onions, add a knob of butter and the mug of rice, give them a bit of a stir.

5) Start measuring 2 mugs worth of the fish stock liquid, add them to the rice and reduce gas mark to the lowest, cover and leave for about 15 minutes.

6) When the rice is nearly cooked, layer the fish on top of the rice and cover.

7) In a little frying pan, add a bit of vegetable oil, and shallow fry the nuts.

8) Serve the rice with the fish and sprinkle some nuts on top, enjoy this dish with any fresh salad or with a Tahini Sauce.

Ingredients for fish stock

1 red mullet with its head

A couple of king prawns with their shells on

1 celery stalk

A couple of cardamoms

Cloves

Salt to taste

2 large onions, chopped

1 bay leaf

2 tsp fish spices (see above).

Method for fish stock

1) Place all in a pot and reduce through boiling.

How to make Tahini Sauce or 'Tarator'

Ingredients

1 cup sesame paste

Juice of two lemons

Juice of half an orange

½ cup of tap water

½ bunch of parsley, finely chopped

3 sprigs of spring onions, finely chopped

Couple of finely chopped radishes or red pepper

¼ tsp ground cumin

Sprinkle of ground hot paprika

Salt to taste

Method

1) Add the sesame paste in to a bowl.

2) Add juice of lemon, orange and water. Give it a whisk.

3) Add the chopped parsley, radishes, and onions. (The red peppers finely chopped are optional but I tried it at my parents in law and it kicked the flavours out of the sauce!)

4) Season with salt, paprika and ground cumin.

5) Serve with sayadieh or any other fish dish as it is a great combination.

Stuffed Koussa and Aubergines in Tomato Sauce

This is one of my family's favourites, especially when we all gather round for Sunday lunch. The dish is famously cooked with stuffed vine leaves and lamb necks or bones added *ad hoc*. The history of stuffing vegetables goes back a long way in the Middle East: as far as the Romans, as Apicius gives a recipe for stuffed marrow under the heading of 'in the Alexandrian manner'; this suggests that Alexandria was well known for its gourds. In fact, in modern

Egyptian cuisine 'Mahashi' – a combination of courgettes, egg plants, tomatoes and peppers, all stuffed with rice and minced lamb – is one of the most popular and traditional of dishes. In Lebanon, both courgettes and marrows are stuffed, in fact stuffed medium-sized marrows are extremely popular in the summer. I remember my aunt scrapping off the outer layer of the marrows and then washing it thoroughly and coring it out. The marrows are then stuffed with rice and minced lamb and cooked in tomato sauce, crushed garlic and dry mint. The above information explains how the Lebanese inherited these dishes from ancestral invaders; however, they evolved to become modern and lighter recipes adapted implicitly by every Lebanese household.

Ingredients

1kg little zucchinis or baby courgettes

1kg little long aubergines

1.5kg lamb necks

500g minced lamb

200g cup of easy cook rice

3 tbsp butter

1 tin chopped tomato

5 tbsp tomato puree

1 tsp salt

1 tsp ground cinnamon

Serves 6-8 persons

Method

1) Wash the courgettes and aubergines thoroughly and cut their top stem. With a circular motion start coring out the marrows gently with the corer. (These are mostly found in Middle Eastern shops like The Green Valley in Edgware Road).

2) Note: for the aubergines, you need to roll it using your palm to soften its interior and make it easy to core out.

3) Put them in a sieve under cold water for a thorough clean and then let them drain for about 20 minutes.

4) In a bowl, mix the minced lamb and rice together, add half of the chopped tomatoes and mix again altogether until the flavours are spread evenly.

5) Season this stuffing with salt and cinnamon to taste.

6) Prepare a large pot, layer the lamb cutlets in it and add the rest of the chopped tomatoes.

7) Start stuffing the courgettes and egg plants; layer them on top of the lamb cutlets. Always layer the aubergines in first because with their harder skin they can cook better. Add the courgettes on top.

8) Mix the tomato puree with a litre of water, season with more salt and ground cinnamon and pour into the pot to cover the courgettes. You may add more water if it's not covered.

9) Compress the ingredients down with plate and cover. Let it boil on high heat, then reduce heat to gas mark 1.

10) Leave to cook for about 90 minutes and then serve with fresh natural yoghurt.

This is a heavenly dish worth all the effort and a great way to entertain your guests or family on any occasion.

Makloobet Batinjan

This is where seduction and I meet face to face, making love to the aubergine itself, topping it with pine kernels, almonds, pistachios and walnuts. These nuts are rich with oils and create a delicious explosion on your palette.

Ingredients

1kg aubergines

3 tomatoes finely chopped

3 onions finely chopped

3 finely chopped garlic cloves

500g lamb cubes (dice into mini ones) or sliced lamb
steaks (my favourite)

1 mug of easy cook rice

50g pine kernels

50g almonds, peeled and cut in half. (Whole almonds
are probably more popular to find, you can boil them
for 10 minutes as they become easier to peel off and
split in half.)

1 tsp ground cinnamon

Salt to season

1.5 tsp of ground all spice

1 cup of basmati rice

Method

1) Wash the aubergines thoroughly and slice them to about 2 cm in thickness. Season with salt and leave to rest for 10 minutes.

2) In the deep oil you can start frying the aubergine slices. Only cook till they are golden, then place them on kitchen paper to drain from excess oil.

3) Rinse the rice under warm water and put in a sieve.

4) Finely chop the onions, tomatoes and garlic.

5) Into a medium size pot bring a bit of sunflower oil to heat. Start by sautéing the onions, garlic and tomatoes until they are golden brown.

6) Add the diced lamb and cook all together for about 10 minutes.

7) Add the fried aubergines into the pot, followed by the rice. Leave on the heat for about 3 minutes, season with a bit more salt and the 1 tbsp of ground cinnamon.

8) Add 2 mugs of hot boiling water to cover the ingredients, put on low heat and allow to cook for around 20-30 minutes.

9) Separately into a frying pan, heat a bit of oil and sauté the pine nuts and almonds until golden; these you can sprinkle on the top of the dish later on when served, or you can leave in a separate plate in case guests or family members have any form of allergy.

10) When through, you can turn it upside down into a dish. Sometimes people like to add carrots and onions to these ingredients, but due to my absolute divine love for this dish I have decided to give it the ultimate taste through the outlined ingredients only;as they say, 'less is more'.

Masbahat El Darwish

The dish presents the food of the poor. 'Darwish' comes from the Turkish word for 'humble and poor'; this clearly shows the Turkish influence on the Lebanese.

'Darweesh' often refers to the poor person, while 'Masbahat' could have double meanings here: either that of swimming (in other words vegetables are drowned into the sauce) or 'Masbaha' is the beaded chain used by religious people for prayers (Christians or Muslims or any other religions). So the dish refers to the vegetables composed in a medley together and drowned into this pool of tomato sauce for the 'Darweesh' or the poor. On the other hand, it could also refer to the medley of vegetables as a symbol of the beaded chain for prayers.

I lay this analysis for you to chose whatever convinces you more; all in all it is a great dish, highly nutritious and very popular, as the dish evolved to include lamb cubes and be eaten with rice.

Ingredients

200g courgettes
200g aubergines
200g potatoes
200gcarrots
200g onions
200g tomatoes
350g lamb cubes (optional)
3 tbsp tomato puree
30g butter
Salt and ground cinnamon
500g lamb cubes (optional)

Method

1) Wash all the vegetables thoroughly and chop them into thick slices.

2) It is entirely up to you if you prefer it with lamb cubes; if so, you can boil the lamb cubes separately with quarter of an onion, salt and black pepper.

3) In a deep roasting tray, add a drizzle of olive oil and the butter. Seal the vegetables for about 10 minutes, stirring from time to time.

4) Separately mix the tomato puree with 350ml of water, salt and ground cinnamon and pour into the vegetables tray. Add the lamb cubes too.

5) Cook in the oven at gas mark 200 °C for about 30 minutes, covered with silver foil.

6) It is best served with rice; sometimes people prefer to eat it just with Arabic bread.

Samke Harra

Ingredients

1 whole large fish, cleaned

2 bunches parsley

3 bunches of spring onions

1.5 bunches of corriander

1kg vine tomatoes

Juice of 4 lemons

2 tsp ground coriander

2 tsp ground cumin

1 tsp ground cinnamon

Salt, according to taste

100ml extra virgin olive oil

Method

1) Wash all the vegetables thoroughly and chop finely into a large bowl.

2) Juice the lemon and mix it with seasoning and olive oil evenly into the salad (stuffing).

3) Season the fish with salt, black pepper and some fish spices (usually found in many ethnic or Middle Eastern shops).

4) Put the fish in a large roasting tray, add some olive oil and try to seal it on the stove. This may take around 10 minutes on each side, due to the size of the fish.

5) Stuff the vegetables into the the fish all the way through and place the rest surrounding the fish, add all the juices and cover with silver foil.

6) Place in the oven at 200 °C for about an hour and a half or until thoroughly cooked; this may differ from one oven to the other and is also affected by the fish's size.

7) Serve the fish meat on a bed of the cooked vegetables, or dig in as you like!!!.

8) Tahini sauce or 'TARATOR' is very popular with fish; see previous recipes.

Laban Emo

Ingredients

1 Lamb shoulder, deboned and cut into large cubes

5 Spanish onions

1.5kg natural yoghurt

2 tbsp corn flour (thickening agent)

1.5 tsp ground cinnamon

⅓ tsp ground cardamoms

½ tsp seven spices

1 tbsp salt

Method

1) Chop the onions finely and sweat them in a pot with some olive oil and vegetable oil.

2) Once the onions are nearly golden add the lamb cubes and stir from time to time until the lamb is sealed; this should take around 8 minutes. add some salt and all the spices.

3) Pour over about 1 litre of hot water and let it cook until the lamb is soft and tender.

4) In the meantime, pour the yoghurt in a bowl and whisk using the hand blender with some salt to taste.

5) Once the lamb cubes are thoroughly cooked, take about 1 cup of the stock with some of the onions and add them. Whizz the onions with the hand blender until they are dissolved in the yoghurt.

6) NB Get rid of the whole stock and keep the lamb cubes in the same pot as you are going to use it again.

7) Mix the cornflour with a bit of water and add them to the yoghurt and mix for 2 minutes.

8) Pour everything back to the pot all with the lamb cubes and bring to boiling point, maintain for 5 minutes and *voilà* the dish is over.

9) This dish is best served with rice pilau; see previous recipe for spinach stew.

Malfoof Mehshi

Cabbage is an excellent autumn ingredient. Apart from its healthy benefits the taste is divine, especially with both lemon and garlic. Cabbage has been cooked by the Romans: both Pliny and Apicius spoke about it in their books. In fact, Sally Grainger, in her book *Cooking Apicius*, mentioned a recipe of spring cabbage with cumin. The latter is miles different from the Lebanese stuffed cabbage; however, stuffing and rolling rice and meat into leaves has been popular in Egypt and Rome and with the Greeks too. As they all happily long settled in the Land of White, the Lebanese again adopted their version of rolling these leaves (vine, swiss chard, cabbage) with rice and vegetables or rice and meat. For this reason I have gone back to my Lebanese roots and decided to prepare this delicious recipe.

Ingredients

1 large Middle Eastern cabbage (usually found in
   Turkish or any Middle Eastern shops)

400g minced lamb

200g long grain rice

Juice of 2 lemons

1 garlic bulb

15g dried mint

2 tsp salt

2 tsp ground cinnamon

4 tbsp extra virgin olive oil

30g of unsalted butter

500g lamb cutlets to place as a first layer at the bottom
   of the pot

Method

1) First bring a big pot of water to the boil with some salt.

2) In the meantime, make a square cut at the top of the cabbage
   around the stem. This way you can start peeling the cabbage leaves
   slowly and neatly. They may tear a little bit but it's okay as you can
   play with them as you like later on.

3) Once the water is boiling, you may start blanching the cabbage
   leaves for five minutes and then place in a sieve.

The stuffing

1) Wash the rice with some warm water and leave in a sieve on the side.

2) In a bowl place the minced lamb, 30g of the butter, salt to taste, 1 tsp ground cinnamon and add the rice. Mix the stuffing all together to spread the flavours evenly.

3) Put some cabbage leaves at the bottom of the pot, then add the lamb cutlets. This is where you will start laying the rolled cabbage leaves.

4) On a board, place the blanched cabbage leaf, cut it in the middle to remove the stem and make it into two pieces, place some stuffing in (average equivalent to 2 tsp depending on the size of the leaf) and now just roll it up like a cigar.

5) Place the rolled cabbage leaf in the pot directly on the bed of lamb cutlets.

6) Peel the garlic bulb and crush it with a pinch of salt; now spread this in the pot all over the wrapped up cabbage leaves.

7) Squeeze the lemons and pour into the pot, add a drizzle of extra virgin olive oil, dry mint, more salt to taste.

8) Cover with warm water and a knob of butter, add heatproof dish on top of the cabbage leaves to press them all down, and cover.

9) Let it cook on gas mark 6; once it boils reduce the heat to 1 and let it cook slowly for about 2 hours.

10) Serve on a plate with some Arabic bread and a selection of fresh spring onions and radish.

Kafta bil Sinneyeh

Ingredients

455g kafta (minced lamb mixed with finely chopped onions and parsley seasoned with salt and ground cinnamon)

300g potatoes

250g onions

250g tomatoes

3 tbsp tomato puree

1 tbsp of butter

Salt

Ground cinnamon

Method

1) Wash all the vegetables thoroughly before you proceed.

2) Peel the onions and potatoes and cut into 1 cm thick slices.

3) Slice the tomatoes in the same way.

4) In a baking tray, bring the kafta mixture and make them into small round balls and put them all around the tray.

5) Add a layer of the sliced potatoes, onions and then the tomatoes.

6) In a separate bowl mix the tomato puree with water; the water has to be enough to cover the ingredients in the tray so you may have to add a bit more of tomato puree or a bit more of water, however you feel you need to.

7) Season with both salt and ground cinnamon.

8) Pour into the baking tray, add the butter and leave in the oven on mark 200°C for about 20-25 minutes; you may have to cover with layer of silver foil to give it more room to steam the sliced potatoes.

9) Eat with Arabic bread.

Riz Bil Foul

This is a great Lebanese dish made in different variations, some with minced lamb and pine kernels, others with just onions; however, my favourite is the former served with tender lamb shank. It is incredibly fascinating to me how same ingredients or even national dishes differ from one region to another or even one household to another.

The story of Riz Bil Foul is so dear to me. Within two months of my marriage I was so proud to cook my version of this dish. Unfortunately my husband Ali thought it was a lousy one as it contained only the basic ingredients of green beans, minced lamb and rice all simmered! A week later he introduced his even more boring version which was only onions, green beans and rice and the amazing part is *he loved it.* YAA, it's a male thing.

Due to my openness to different cultures and food habits, I decided to step up to the challenge and create my own version that everyone is going to like and here it is presented and shared with all of you.

What I love about these rice dishes is the freedom to use my own flavoured stocks. I love lamb shanks: there is something magical about the aroma and flavours of them boiled with aromatics, such as half stem of leeks, a carrot, half an onion, a sprig of celery, some cloves and couple of cardamoms, salt and cinnamon to taste. You have the choice to enhance the flavours however you like.

Ingredients

4 lamb shanks (boiled separately)

500g green beans

1 mug of easy cook rice

250g minced lamb

1 tsp salt or to taste

1 tsp ground black pepper

1 tsp ground cinnamon

½ tsp ground cumin

2 mugs of lamb shank stock while at boiling point

50g pine kernels sautéed with a knob of butter

50g almonds peeled and sautéed with a knob of butter

Method

1) While the lamb shank is cooking in boiling water with the aromatics and seasoning, you can start your amazing rice dish.

2) In a pot, add a drizzle of vegetable oil or a knob of butter, add the minced lamb and sautée until thoroughly cooked.

3) Add the frozen green beans or fresh ones, whatever you prefer, and keep stirring. At this point lower the heat to minimum, cover with lid and let the beans and minced lamb steam cook for about 10 minutes while stirring from time to time.

4) Add the rice and season with 2 tsp ground cinnamon, a dash of ground black pepper, ground cumin and salt to taste.

5) Add 2 mugs' worth of lamb shank stock into the rice, give it a bit of a stir, leave it on minimum heat and put the lid back on. Leave to simmer for about 15 to 20 minutes, until rice is thoroughly cooked.

6) In a hot pan, add the knobs of butter and stir in both pine kernels and almonds until golden brown.

7) Serve the rice with some lamb shank strips and throw some nuts on top: heavenly with salad or natural yoghurt.

Moloukhieh wa Ruz

This is one of the most famous and important recipes in the Middle East; everyone tends to cook it in a different way and claims theirs as the original one.

Molokhia or Moloukieh is a mucilaginous, nutritious type of greens, also known as Jew's mallow (as well as Nalta jute, Tussa jute, Corchorus olitorius), which is found throughout Egypt, the Levant, and similar climes elsewhere. It used to be a hugely expensive ingredient eaten only by the Egyptian kings or pharoahs: hence it was known as 'Moloukieh' which comes from the word 'Molook', plural of 'king'. Others believe that this dish was first prepared by the ancient Israelites.

Jew's mallow is usually cooked with chicken or lamb cubes, garlic, onions, coriander, chilli peppers and a squeeze of lemon juice served with rice.

Ingredients

1kg of dry Jew's mallow or Molokhieh (this can be found
  in any Middle Eastern shop)
1 baby chicken (poussin) or 1kg of lamb cubes
1 large Spanish onion
2 bulbs of garlic, peeled
1 or 2 hot peppers (optional)
1 bunch of fresh coriander
30ml of sunflower or vegetable oil
Salt and cinnamon to season
1½ lemons

Method

1) In a pot bring the lamb cubes or the baby chicken to boil. As usual please do not forget to season with salt, cinnamon, black peppercorn and an onion to remove any odours.

2) Open the Jew's mallow bag and try to remove the bottom stem: this is an important part of the cooking process as it removes the mucus substance from the stem which is released when is cooked. This is the hardest part of the recipe!

3) When you finished removing the bottom stem you can now bring to boil with the juice of a half lemon and sprinkle of salt.

4) Peel the garlic and set on the side. Wash the fresh coriander thoroughly, remove the bunch's stems and chop roughly.

5) Peel the large onion, wash it thoroughly and dry and on the stove bring it to grill on all sides.

6) Once ready, put the garlic, grilled onion and coriander (in addition to the optional ingredients of hot and sweet pepper) into the food processor. Process until mixture becomes fine: not necessarily like a puree but finely chopped.

7) You may have to check the Jew's mallow now: the leaves should look or appear fresh green similar to spinach. Even if they are half boiled that does not matter as they are going to be cooked further. Sieve them and leave aside.

8) Check your lamb cubes or the chicken: if they are thoroughly cooked leave on the side and keep the stock as it will be used for the stew. If you have chosen the chicken option you need to de-bone it.

9) The fun part is finally here: add the cooking oil and the Jew's mallow to a pot. Stir slowly on medium,

10) Add the onion and garlic mixture and stir again; this process should last about 5-8 minutes as you can enjoy the garlic and coriander's aroma while cooking.

11) You can now add the lamb cubes or chicken and stir a bit more, top it up with the stock and allow to cook on low fire for about 25-30 minutes.

12) Best served with rice a squeeze of lemon juice and Arabic bread.

You may have noticed that the presentation of this dish is completely different from the Egyptian and Sudanese way as they would normally chop the leaves finely and cook with onions: the texture becomes more of a slimy soup eaten with rice. It is also known that the Egyptians eat it with rabbits rather than chicken or lamb; I can confess here that the procedure may have descended from the oldest method of cooking herbs or leaves (chopping it finely or even pounding it which is still a common procedure in both Africa and India). Although the Lebanese acquired the dish from the Egyptians they have added to it a complete new flavour and aroma; the Egyptians served it with some toasted bread and onions soaked in vinegar. The Egyptians are well known for using rabbits in their Jew's mallow stews; the Lebanese use tender lamb cubes or a baby chicken. It is not very common to eat rabbits in Lebanon or Syria anyway.

Moghrabiye

'*Moghrabiye*' (also *moghrabie*, *moghrabieh*) is the Moroccan word for 'feminine' or 'lady'. I believe the North African variety of couscous is differentiated from the Lebanese in its making and presentation. The former looks more like crushed wheat however, the latter is made from durum wheat and soaked with water and egg to make it like little soft pasta beads. People would often mistake it to pasta beads and the taste is rather bland so it requires a lot of spices or strong flavours to enhance its being.

The Lebanese cuisine is a result of all the many invasions of the land. People were open to many other cultures and exchanged methods and ingredients of cooking. The close relation between North Africa and Sicilian food throughout history ultimately demonstrates why the Lebanese eat spaghetti (Makarona) and also why we made our durum wheat into tiny beaded balls, ready to be steamed with some caraway and other spices.

The major and most overwhelming spice in the moghrabiye is the caraway, and then come the other aromatics used in the lamb and chicken stock.

In Beirut, people buy fresh moghrabiye from the shop in the same way as we buy fresh pasta from supermarkets here in the West.

Ingredients

1kg packet of dried moghrabiye

1 chicken quartered and boiled with aromatics (sprig of celery, 1 carrot, 1 onion, sprig of leeks, bay leaf, clovers and cardamom and some caraway)

1kg lamb cubes boiled thoroughly with aromatics (onions, ground cinnamon, celery, leeks, bay leaf, carrot, clovers, cardamom)

2 cans of chickpeas, washed and drained

1kg shallots, peeled

2 tsp ground caraway

2 tsp ground cinnamon

A dash of white pepper

2 tbsp butter (to toss the moghrabiye)

1.5 litres of water

Method

1) Put the quartered chicken into a pot of water, add its aromatics and bring it to boil until it is thoroughly tender. This may take about 45 minutes. Apply the same method to the lamb cubes at the same time.

2) Once the lamb and chicken are tender allow to cool, but preserve both stocks in beakers.

3) In a pot of boiling salted water, add the moghrabiye pearls and cook until tender: this will take for about 20 minutes. Remove pot from heat and pour the moghrabiye into a colander and wash under cold running water.

4) In a clean pot, put some butter and add the peeled shallots and cook until golden.

5) Add the moghrabiye to the golden shallots and stir every 3 minutes. Season with ground caraway, ground cinnamon and salt to taste.

6) Add the drained chickpeas and reduce the heat and keep mixing them all together.

7) Add the lamb and chicken stock to the moghrabiye pearls and let it simmer (100ml).

8) Preserve the rest of the hot stock as an extra on the side, because the pearls absorb the liquid quickly and you will always need extra sauce on the side. Leave the lamb cubes and chicken together with some of the onions, but take out all the other aromatics.

Ablama Koussa

'Ablama' is a word beyond my explanation, I have tried to use other sources as to explain the word and why has it been used on such a distinctive dish as sophisticated as this one.

'Abla' in Turkish and Egyptian means 'the old sister' and could have been what the old sister at home cooked for the family or even in shelter homes, where the carer was referred to as 'Abla' too.

Originally this dish is Turkish: it descends from other aubergine dishes cooked with minced lamb and pine nuts. The region (both Lebanon and Syria were one country on the map) was ruled by the Ottomans for nearly 400 years and obviously Aleppo in Syria and other regions were highly influenced by this rule.

The dish itself comprises stuffed baby courgettes with minced lamb and pine nuts in tomato sauce. As mentioned earlier the Lebanese always took this further the extra mile! I am not biased; this is the nature of the people in this part of the region.

Ablama has indeed evolved to become a sophisticated, first class dish; over the years people have cooked it on its own without rice and added more tantalizing and mouthwatering flavours to it.

I remember my grandmother serving it in a deep stainless steel tray full of baby courgettes, fairly small potatoes and artichoke hearts. They were all pre-fried and sieved to remove the extra oil until they were cool. Then they were stuffed with minced lamb and nuts and all cooked with crushed garlic, lemon juice and extra virgin olive oil. My grandmother served this dish with rice pilaf because she had a large family; on the other hand this was not the case with smaller families or how the dish was served in classical restaurants.

The recipe evolved from being just baby courgettes with minced lamb and pine nuts in tomato sauce to that of baby courgette, artichoke hearts, potatoes and tomatoes, by adding a lighter combination of garlic, lemon juice and olive oil. Following some field research and observation of the regional recipes, the comparison I draw is of turning around what was essentially a tomato sauce and garlic and coriander combination found in many of the stews into a garlic, lemon juice and olive oil combination. If one looks at potato stew, it was done with tomato sauce and garlic and then twisted to the fresher flavours. The same applies to stuffed cabbage: many people in the mountains and southern villages cook this recipe with tomato sauce and garlic; in Beirut, by contrast, people tend to prefer the lighter version of garlic and lemon juice. The list of such recipes is endless. This could be related to the weather, so we have tomato sauce in stews for winter and garlic with lemon juice and coriander in the summer.

Ingredients

1kg small courgettes
500g artichoke hearts (frozen)
500g fairly small potatoes
500g fairly small tomatoes
8 cloves of garlic, crushed
Juice of 3 lemons
80ml extra virgin olive oil
2 tbsp pomegranate molasses
2 cups of water
Salt to taste
Vegetable oil for deep-frying

Ingredients for the Stuffing

500g minced lamb or beef, whatever is your desire
180g pine nuts
1 tsp ground cinnamon
Salt to taste
20ml vegetable oil or just spray

Method

1) Wash the vegetables thoroughly and pat dry, peel the potatoes and with a corer dig deep inside and make a hole for the stuffing. Do the same to the tomato without peeling it and set aside.

2) Take the baby courgettes and cut the top stem and slowly remove its circular bottom. Core the courgettes and wash well again.

3) Deep fry the courgettes, artichokes, potatoes and tomatoes until tender and slightly golden. Place on absorbent paper to get rid of excess oil.

4) In the meantime, take a separate frying pan and spray with a bit of oil, add the pine nuts and toss for couple of minutes,then add the mince and cook for about ten minutes all together or until tender. Add the salt and ground cinnamon and let it rest to cool down.

5) Once cooled down, spoon the mince stuffing into the courgettes, tomatoes, potatoes and artichoke. Arrange this medley into your desired oven dish, and pour over the crushed garlic, lemon juice, olive oil and pomegranate molasses alongside the 2 cups of water.

6) Add the salt to taste and put in the oven at 180°C for about 40 minutes. For best results cover with foil.

7) This dish is very healthy and can be enjoyed just on its own, the citrus flavours enriching the dry texture of the artichokes and the garlic with the olive oil when tasting the potatoes are just irresistible. It is indeed a luxurious dish on its own but with kids, I bet serving it with rice pilaf would do the trick; kids find it hard to resist potatoes and rice.

My Tip

1) You may choose to cook this dish with tomato sauce and all you have to do is pour a can of tomato puree into a bowl, add 3 cups of water and some salt, a tsp of black pepper, 2 tsp ground cinnamon and pour over the stuffed vegetables. Cover with foil and cook in the oven at 180°C for about 45 minutes and serve with rice pilaf. This is a heavier and the older version of the recipe and is better served with rice; in my opinion this is still more popular in commercial restaurants and among larger families.

2) Ablama with lemon and garlic is sophisticated and its luxurious ingredients tempt you to eat it just *solo*.

Lamb Shank and the Five Spices

Ingredients

4 lamb shanks

Aromatics: 1 onion, ½ celery, ½ leek, 1 carrot

Spices:

Couple of whole cardamom, semi crushed or 1 tsp of
  ground cardamom

Couple of whole cloves or 1 tsp ground cloves

1 tsp ground cumin

1 tsp ground black pepper

1 tsp ground cinnamon

Ingredients of the Rice

250g minced lamb

100g pine nuts

100g whole almonds

100g pistachios

2 cups of basmati rice

Same quantity of spices applied again

4 cups of boiling stock water

Method

1) In a hot pot, add a drizzle of vegetable oil and all the nuts; stir them
   gently until semi golden in colour. Add the minced lamb and keep
   stirring until it is thoroughly cooked.

2) Add the rice and keep stirring, add the tablespoons of each of the
   spices and stir again.

3) Add the required boiling liquid from the lamb shanks' stock
   and keep the rice on really low heat with the lid on for about 20
   minutes.

4) Serve the rice with a lamb shank and some natural yoghurt or fresh salad.

Rice and lamb or chicken dishes are often the main dish for dinner or lunch parties. They are easy and accept any form of spice mix to add an extra flavour to both the rice and type of meat included. Many people prefer grilled baby chicken with the rice, others prefer leg of lamb or even a whole grilled lamb.

I believe these dishes are Arabic in origin, meaning from the Bedouin style of popular rice dishes like the traditional 'Arabian Mansaf' and the Saudi dishes of 'Kabse'. These are rice dishes enlivened with any sort of meat (chicken, lamb, camel, mutton, ducks or pigeons); however, adding the different spice mix and some raisins and dates creates a whole different taste and gastronomical experience.

In Kuwait and UAE, people enjoy camel meat with the rice, accompanied by camel's milk as a drink. The rice is served in large circular stainless steel or brass trays with the pieces of meat and nuts all laying on the top of the rice. Natives enjoy these meals gathered around the circular tray and eating by their hands.

All in all, among the most popular rice dishes for the Lebanese is the 'Totbika' which is the boiled baby chicken and the minced lamb; others prefer lamb shoulder or even large tender lamb cubes. Personally, I love this dish because it is easy to do, nutritionally balanced as a main meal and the kids just love it whether with a dollop of natural yoghurt or even simple salad.

Leg of Lamb with Saffron Rice

Ingredients for the leg of lamb

1 leg of lamb

10 cloves of garlic, peeled

2 tsp salt

1 tsp black pepper

1 tsp ground cinnamon

½ tsp ground cardamom

½ tsp ground cumin

½ tsp ground coriander

40ml olive oil

Method for the Leg of Lamb

1) Rest the leg of lamb on your worktop.

2) Using a knife, make holes all over it, to put the peeled garlic cloves.

3) Rub the spices and seasoning all over it, and massage the lamb with the olive oil.

4) Place in a roasting tray and put on the cooker on medium heat to lock the flavour in all around, a process about 8 minutes on each side.

5) Leave in the same tray, add around 250ml water, cover with tin foil and leave in the oven at 180°C for about 2 ½ hours or until thoroughly cooked.

Note: it genuinely depends on the type of oven one has. Some will require three hours and some only two.

Rice with Saffron

250g basmati rice

½ tsp ground turmeric

½ tsp saffron, stirred in 2 tbsp orange blossom water

1 mistika, ground

Salt to season

Squadge of cooking liquid to stir the rice

500 ml of hot boiling water

3 Spanish onions, peeled and sliced into trenches, cooked with some oil separately until golden brown to use on top of the rice

Tip: When you put the onions in oil add some saffron to them, about 4 threads, to add that yellow colour.

Method

1) Start your kettle for hot water.

2) Add the cooking liquid into the pot and when it starts to bubble, add the rice.

3) Stir fry the rice and add the turmeric, saffron with the rose water and salt.

4) Add the 500ml of hot boiling water, allow to simmer on gas mark 1 for about 15 minutes.

5) Serve with golden brown onions on top and leg of lamb on the side, eaten with either salad or yoghurt.

6) You may also add some toasted almonds and pine nuts as that will add to its crunchiness.

Djaj Bil Toom

Ingredients

1kg chicken thighs, all cleaned with lemon juice and salt under cold water

500g jersey potatoes

1 bulb garlic, peeled

120ml vegetable oil

2 free range egg whites

Salt to taste

Method

1) The first step into this favourite dish is to make the garlic sauce or *toom*.

2) Put the peeled garlic cloves into the food processor with a dash of salt and blitz.

3) Start adding the vegetable oil slowly and thinly from the little tip at the top of the processor and let it blitz for about 10 minutes.

4) Now add the egg whites and carry on with the rest of the vegetable oil being poured in slowly until they all coagulate together and forms a silky and creamy texture.

5) Apply about 3 tbsp of this mixture to the raw chicken along with the juice of a lemon and some salt.

6) Add the washed potatoes into the baking tray and let it cook in the oven at 220°C for about 30 minutes.

7) Turn them around within 15 minutes to get its top skin crispy; you may fork them a bit to release some of its juices.

8) Just enjoy with some extra toom or garlic sauce and fresh green salad. This is the ideal of fast, simple, fresh and delicious!

Yakhnet Banadoora

Vine tomato stew is one of my favourite dishes: it is simple and a definite winter warmer. My aunt's version involves cooking the tomatoes as they are in a baking tray stuffed with minced lamb, pine nuts, crushed garlic and coriander.

On the other hand, my mother would chop the fresh tomatoes, stir fry them for a bit and then simmer with some water and add the garlic and coriander to it. My mother would then scatter cooked minced lamb and pine nuts on the top of the stew before service.

I must admit they both taste lovely, however presentation-wise I still prefer my aunt's version and I usually combine it with pilau rice. The dish itself is not too traditional; it is an adapted dish based on the wide availability of fresh vine tomatoes. Usually it is preferable to use fully ripened tomatoes.

It is more of a Beirutian dish (meaning originally from the city of Beirut). It is quite traditional for people coming from villages at the end of summer to bring some of their land's fresh produce and condiments to exchange or give away as presents to their friends, families and neighbours. Some of this fresh produce could have been tomatoes and families would cook them with garlic and coriander, so tomato stew has become a dish adapted from other similar vegetable stews.

Ingredients

4 good sized ripened vine tomatoes

200g minced lamb

40g pine nuts

2 cloves garlic crushed

½ bunch fresh coriander, finely chopped

2 tbsp tomato puree

Dash of vegetable oil

1 tsp ground cinnamon

Salt to taste

Method

1) Wash the tomatoes thoroughly, core it using the apple corer and then close its bottom with a little piece of the tomato. Place them in the desired baking dish.

2) In the meantime, add a dash of oil into a hot pan and stir fry the minced lamb and the nuts. Season with some salt and ground cinnamon.

3) Using a teaspoon, add the minced lamb mix into each of the tomatoes and then sprinkle the rest around the tomatoes in the baking dish.

4) Into the same pan, add another dash of salt and stir fry the crushed garlic and fine coriander for about 2 minutes, then scatter all over the tomato dish.

5) Add the tomato puree and around 250ml hot water, season with salt to taste and let it bake in the oven at 200°C for about 15 -20 minutes, or until the tomatoes are thoroughly cooked but still maintain their shape.

6) It is best eaten with pilau rice or just flat Arabic bread.

ARABIC DESSERTS

THE LEBANON HAS been an attractive strategic region for many invaders over the time. The Romans and the Greeks translated their influence through ruins of Baalbeck or the Sun City. The Phoenicians, known as top world adventurers and business dealers, were the native settlers in the city-states of Tyre and Sidon. Assyrians imposed their love of food and exquisite banquets, then there were the Egyptians and the Ottomans and last but not least the French Mandate that ended in 1921. Lebanon gained its final independence and recognition as a country in 1946.

Although these were settlers who aimed for power, politics and conflict, the positive outcome was the cultural exchange they brought with them: the style of dressing, language influences and behavioural etiquette, in addition to ingredients and spices that were adopted into the Lebanese's daily dishes and have since become distinctive to the Land of White itself.

Tabbouleh for example is the Lebanese national salad; however, the Turks present it with cucumbers and carrots. I am not too sure whether I can accept that in my tabbouleh as a Lebanese and whether it is related to a subjective reason or purely scientific one; that carrots and cucumbers are too crunchy and bulky for such a finely chopped salad texture.

The Ottomans left us a lot of their desserts. Osmanlieh is shredded long vermicelli soaked with ghee, rose water and stuffed with clotted cream. Eish El Saray is a similar dessert, made of semolina this time but also stuffed with clotted cream or even the choice of pounded nuts as pistachios with sugar and rose water. As a country rich with its food and cultural background, the French were generous too: we inherited petit fours and many cakes. In fact, top patisseries in Lebanon are highly reputable for the quality and creativity of their cakes. A great selection of the French influence has been traditionally presented in these cake houses and among this selection are petit fours, swiss rolls, boule au chocolat and tarte au fraise and forêt noir or black forest.

In this chapter, I will be considering first the dishes with Middle Eastern influence and then, in the next section, the European recipes. I hope you enjoy them as they really descend from a huge selection of what both my mum and my aunt used to bake for us at home and others we used to buy from specialist shops with the ability to re-create at home. After all, my family members are sweet lovers.

Maakaroun

Ingredients

1.5 cup fine semolina

2.5 cup self raising flour

½ cup rose water

¾ cup vegetable oil

½ cup milk

3 tbsp aniseed

 2 tbsp sesame seeds

Vegetable oil for deep-frying

Serves 10 persons and more

Method

1) Mix all the dry ingredients together.

2) Add the vegetable oil, milk and rose water.

3) Mix and knead until you get a good sized dough; the texture should be well held together and not an elastic one.

4) Make little balls of the dough.

5) Using a sieve, place the ball on it, flatten it with your fingers and then roll it like a cigar.

6) Deep fry in the vegetable oil until dark golden. Let it cool and sieve to remove excess oil.

7) Throw into a bowl of sugar syrup and then place in a serving platter with a garnish of ground pistachios or more sesame seeds.

Layali Lubnan – Lebanese Nights

A traditional semolina and milk pudding, topped with ashta (clotted cream), ground nuts and sugar syrup.

Semolina and honey pudding was mentioned by Apicius; I believe that is where the whole Middle Eastern region originally acquired such combinations, but this has developed into varied forms.

For example, there is a similar milk pudding made of milk and corn starch and then set in the fridge for couple of hours, served also with nuts and sugar syrup. This is known as 'Mohalabie' and nowadays it's quite popular to serve it with concentrated fruit syrups such as strawberry or mulberry.

Another popular pudding uses rice; again it is a similar content but adding rice as the substitute for corn starch. However, the rice pudding does not require any form of syrup because the recipe contains a lot of sugar, giving the rice the time to cook with the milk and absorb the sugar then coagulate all together.

Layali Lubnan or Lebanese Nights is a similar combination, but an easier option because once you set the milk to boiling point, the fine semolina is added and this thickens the texture as long as you are whisking on moderate heat. The mix is then emptied into ramekins, glass serve ware or any other similarly-sized dish as you desire. Once cooled and allowed to set in the fridge for about three hours it is then topped with clotted cream or double cream and nuts.

Ingredients

4 cups of full fat milk

1 cup fine semolina

½ cup caster sugar

20ml rose water

20ml orange blossom water

Couple of mistikas (pounded with a sprinkle of sugar)

200ml double cream, to be whipped

50g ground pistachios

50g orange blossom petals preserve (optional)

Method

1) Bring the milk and the sugar to the boil while whisking slowly from time to time, especially around the edges of the pot.

2) Add the pounded mistika, orange blossom and rose water.

3) Once it reaches boiling point, add the semolina and keep whisking at low moderate heat.

4) This is a critical stage: you should whisk it continuously until the mixture thickens thoroughly.

5) Empty into your desired glassware and cool for about 90 minutes, then place in the fridge to set for about 2 hours.

6) In the meantime, whip the double cream and ground the pistachios and prepare the sugar syrup or use honey, whichever is more convenient for you. For sugar syrup use the recipe on the following pages.

7) Once the pudding is set, spread the double cream evenly on top and then sprinkle the ground nuts and some of the orange blossom petals preserve. Serve with sugar syrup and enjoy the fresh and fragrant taste of milk with nuts and mistika. It is a taste of heaven, absolutely voluptuous.

Namoura

A dessert made of semolina soaked with butter and milk, then baked. The Egyptians has a similar base known as 'Basbousa' all soaked with sugar syrup and some flavoured with coconuts too. I keep wondering where the name 'Namoura' came from and, since it has the same base as the 'Basbousa', why different names were used in the same Arabic or Middle Eastern region. The former, 'Namoura', probably descends from the word 'Amoura', which comes in turn from the word 'Amour', meaning love. The Lebanese would have bought this from a lovely lady on the streets and called it 'Amoura' in local Lebanese, meaning cute and lovely; this could have been a sweet baked base and something one bought from the 'Amoura Lady'; over the years the 'N' could have been added to give it a hidden definition. 'Basbousa' has the same kind of meaning in Egypt, it comes from the word 'Bessa', a cat, and again this could be the same case applied here: namoura being sold by a lovely pussy cat and Tom Jones was the customer!

All in all and after careful consideration and reading, I can say the origins of this cake is that of an Egyptian base. After all, Ancient Egyptians were among the first in the world to experiment with baking with yeast and kneading dough with their feet and baking cakes.

If I wanted to become a bit more sceptical and add some philosophy to this, 'Amoura' might have descended from the Ancient Egyptian gods 'Amon' and 'Ra' and maybe baking these combinations in the ancient world was presented to the gods and pharaohs to keep them happy in the underworld. Anyhow, who cares? We just want to say thank you to our ancestors, whether the Romans, Egyptians or the Greeks, for the fantastic base recipes we inherited from them. They are scrumptious.

Ingredients

2½ cups of semolina

125g unsalted butter

1 cup caster sugar

1 x can evaporated milk

20ml orange blossom water

20ml rose water

Almond nuts for decoration

500ml of sugar syrup (see page 164 for sugar syrup
  recipe.)

Method

1) Put the sugar, semolina and butter into a large tray and mix well with your hands. Use the rubbing motion for at least 10 minutes until you the feel the sugar has dissolved into the mixture.

2) Add the evaporated milk and rub again all together for 10 minutes. Leave to rest for an hour.

3) Rub the mixture again and add the fragranced waters and let it rest for at least 4 hours in dry and warm place.

4) The semolina mix is ready to bake: pat it with the palm of your hands into a round baking tray 30cm and bake in the oven at 160°C for 40 minutes or until golden.

5) Take out the namoura mix. Using a knife start cutting slowly into squares and place the almonds into each square.

6) Allow to cool completely. Add the 500ml of sugar syrup on top of the baked namoura and leave again to rest for an hour at the end of which time the syrup is completely absorbed.

7) Take out in square forms and serve.

Zenood el Set (Lady's Arms)

Originally a puff pastry stuffed with clotted cream and then deep-fried and served with sugar syrup. Many of the Arabic desserts involved puff pastry and clotted cream or even pounded nuts mixed with sugar and fragrant waters. It is known as Lady's arms because it's round and looks perfectly like a beautiful and sexy lady's arm; this reveals the culture of the Middle Eastern region and their appreciation of beauty and passion for both food and beautiful women. There are many other similar desserts known as Kallage which is too popular in Ramadan, the latter's pastry is much thinner and drier pastry. I remember my mum soaking the Kallage pastry in cold milk then stuffing it with clotted cream. She then folded it into a good sized triangle and deep-fried it. All in all, this is my modest recipe that can be enjoyed locally and trust me, it has the same taste and is far easier to make.

Ingredients

20 x spring roll sheets (spring roll sheets, from any
   supermarket or ethnic shops)
500ml vegetable oil for deep-frying

Ingredients for Cream stuffing

5 cups full fat milk
¾ cup corn flour
25ml orange blossom water
25ml rose water
Couple of mistikas pounded in a teaspoon of sugar

Method

1) In a hot pan, pour 4½ cups of milk and let it come to boil.
2) In the meantime mix the cornflour into the ½ cup of remaining milk and set aside.
3) Once the milk starts to boil, reduce the heat and add the corn flour cup. Carry on whisking and add the ground mistika.
4) This is a critical stage: you should whisk quickly, not let it boil. As it thickens, add the blossom and rose water.
5) The mixture should have thickened by now: pour into a bowl and let cool.

For Glueing

4 tbsp corn flour mixed in ½ cup of water (get them to
   boil and thicken)

Assembly

1) On your working top, lay down the pastry sheets.
2) Once the cream is cooled, add 1 ½ tsp into the pastry sheet.
3) Fold on the side and glue with the cornflour and water mixture, then roll it over like a cigarette and glue the end of it.
4) You may let them rest in the fridge for about half an hour.
5) Heat the oil and deep-fry until they are golden.
6) This is best served with sugar syrup.

Halawet el Jeben
(The cheese sweetness)

This is a great dessert. Both melted cheese and clotted cream work wonders together. For this recipe and many others included, you will need sugar syrup and clotted cream. These will be explained in this recipe.

Halawt el Jeben is a traditional dessert native to Tripoli in the Northern regions of the Lebanon. Tripoli is one of the most beautiful cities of the Land of White, with a strategic port famous for fishing and open waters leading to Cyprus. Tripoli is famous in manufacturing excellent quality of pine and walnut woods, people tend to buy the famous Arabic Oud, a traditional instrument made of walnut wood from Tripoli. It is also famous for its Khan El Saboun (Soap Market): the soaps are renowned for their use of natural extra virgin olive oil.

'Al Hallab' a leading name in the making of Halawet el Jeben in Tripoli, is a traditional family business and is now one of the top names in the entire Middle East actually. I remember visiting his shop in 2001, when I had my 'Alicia' restaurant in Warren Street, London. The patisserie served many varied traditional desserts such as Baklawa, Maamoul and most of all the Halawat el Jeben. What attracted me though was the halawet el riz (meaning sweetened rice) which is also done in a similar way. However, I prefer leaving that to the professionals as it is time-consuming. One of my favourites was the 'Jazarieh': carrots cooked and reduced in sugar syrup with walnuts and almonds. It is just mind-blowing. I have seen this dessert recreated by many but Mr Refaat El Halab's is truly number one.

How to make Sugar Syrup

6 cups of caster sugar

3 cups of water

Method

1) Bring the ingredients into a pot and put on heat. Stir until the sugar is dissolved, lower heat to medium and add 2 tbsp orange blossom and 2 tbsp rose water.

2) Squeeze the juice of a half a lemon and let it boil until it becomes sticky.

3) You can check by dipping a spoon in and take it out, let it rest for a minute and then see if it's sticky. When it is, move off the heat and cool down for storage.

How to make Clotted Cream

(To serve 6-8)

1 medium bloomer loaf, cored out and shredded

1½ litre full fat milk

2x 225g extra thick double cream

Couple of mistikas pounded with a pinch of sugar

2 tbsp orange blossom water

2 tbsp rose water

Method

1) Peel the outer crust of the bloomer and tear the soft core into small pieces. Place the torn bread into a deep pot and cover it all with full fat milk, let it rest in the fridge for 24 hours or until it absorbs all the milk.

2) Bring the milk and bread to boil, pound some mistika with a spoon of sugar and add it to the milk. When they reach boiling point add 2 pots of extra thick double cream (2 x 225ml pots).

3) Turn down the heat and stir for a bit, add the blossom and rose water and keep stirring for another 3 minutes.

4) Remove from heat and empty in a container, let it rest and cool down and stir it every 10 minutes, leave for 90 minutes and then place in the fridge. It lasts for about 3 days or according to double creams shelf life.

How to make the Halawa

1kg mozzarella cheese
1 cup fine semolina
1 cup sugar syrup

Method

1) Add the sugar syrup to a non-stick pot or a good quality stainless steel one and bring it to boil.

2) Add the mozzarella cheese and reduce heat slightly. Stir until the cheese starts melting into the syrup and become combined.

3) Add the semolina; keep stirring quickly until the texture becomes an elasticated cheesy dough.

4) Now you may reduce the heat completely, and pour the cheese halawa on a clean and spacious worktop covered with sugar syrup, this will let you work more easily with the halawa.

5) Now start rolling the halawa to make it smooth and flat. You may either cut into thin slices or cut into medium triangles and place the clotted cream and roll like a cigarette.

6) This is best served with extra sugar syrup on the side.

Mafrouke

This is a sweetened semolina base topped with fresh clotted cream and nuts.

Ingredients

2 cups caster sugar

2 cups of cold water

1 cup fine semolina

1 cup coarse semolina

1 tbsp unsalted butter

30ml orange blossom water

30ml rose water

Method

1) In a deep pan, add the two cups of caster sugar and bring to caramel stage. Reduce heat or gas mark to low medium and add the two cups of cold water.

2) This is a critical stage as you have to keep stirring gently and not let the sugar crystals set.

3) Now add the two cups of semolina with the butter and keep stirring.

4) You can now fragrance with orange blossom and rose water while stirring.

5) Empty immediately into your desired flat-shaped dish – whether oval or squared I leave that to you – and spread evenly.

6) Allow to cool and start working on your clotted cream topping.

7) *Note please*: It is extremely difficult and demanding to spread the mafrouke mix when hot. My tip is to use a little bowl of warm water as you dip in the spoon or spatula used every time you spread a little. It is highly preferable that the mafrouke mix is not more than 2 cm thick.

8) Look out for the clotted cream recipe (page 164) and always do it at least 24 hours before making the mafrouke. Spread all over the mafrouke and scatter your desired nuts such as fresh almond halves, pine nuts and pistachios.

9) The freshness of the clotted cream coincides with the sweetness of the mafrouke and just balances the sweetness of the mix; the nuts add an extra crunchy element to the palettes' experience and makes it a worthwhile experience to treat family and friends to.

Sfouf

Ingredients

2 cups of semolina

1 cup of self raising flour

1 cup of vegetable oil

2 cups full fat milk

2 cups caster sugar

1 tsp turmeric

2 tsp baking powder

100g pine nuts

Method

1) Into a bowl empty the dry ingredients and mix together with your hands.

2) Pour the oil and start mixing and milk and use the electric mixer until all combined.

3) Add the turmeric and mix it all again.

4) Line a baking tray (28 cm) with some butter to avoid sticking and pour the batter all in, add the pine nuts randomly into it.

5) Place in a preheated oven at 180°C for about 40 minutes or until thoroughly cooked.

6) Allow to cool, then cut into squares and serve or store in cake tins as it lasts for up to a week.

Note: The word 'Sfouf' itself means 'straight line' and that is exactly how it is presented in all the traditional Middle Eastern sweet shops.

Sanioura

Sanioura is a delicious and scrumptious type of a biscuit circle usually eaten in the Eid or at any celebration. It is familiar to the mountains of Lebanon and the Eastern side mountains where it's made in large quantities and sent to the local bakery for baking.

My grandmother's favourite recipe was sanioura. I remember sitting with her on the blue tiles of the small kitchen and rolling the sanioura into balls and then she rolled it in her hand to a snake shape and close at the ends. It was fun to see the biscuits being cooked and then resist tasting them as I waited for them to cool down before eating.

Ingredients

200g ghee butter

200g icing sugar (sieved)

400g flour (sieved)

100g pistachios for decoration

Method

1) Rub the butter with the icing sugar.

2) Add the sieved flour and rub all together to make a mixture. Let it rest for about an hour in cool dry place.

3) Take a little ball and then roll into a baby snake and then attach both ends. Place one pistachio on the top.

4) Bake in the oven at 160°C for about 12 minutes or until it is thoroughly cooked. (Check at the bottom if its semi golden.)

Rice Pudding (Riz Bil Haleeb)

Ingredients

½ cup arborio rice or rice pudding

3 cups of full fat milk

1 cup of double cream

¼ cup of caster sugar

1 vanilla pod

Method

1) Into a pot pour the milk, double cream and rice and bring into gentle heat.
2) Add the sugar and vanilla pod and keep stirring occasionally.
3) Keep it on medium or gentle heat for about 40 minutes until the rice is thoroughly cooked.

Ingredients and Method for the Strawberry syrup

250g fresh juicy sweet strawberries

50g caster sugar

Juice of 1 lemon

1) Crush the strawberries in blender with the sugar and juice of lemon.
2) Sieve into a pot and simmer on gentle heat until reduced and thick.
3) Allow the mix to cool and pour into your desired glass or bowl then top with the rice pudding and allow it to set in the fridge for about an hour or so. Garnish with some fresh mint.

After some experimental research I decided to include this recipe instead of the traditional one. I found this recipe easier and quicker and less ad hoc, especially as a busy working mum of two. My mum's version that has been directly inherited from her mum involves boiling 1 gallon of full fat milk with rice pudding for an hour or so. It involves pounding mistika and constant stirring to dissolve the sugar and some corn flour to set the milk when it cools. Ouch; I am a working mum of two and there are only 24 hours in the 24 hours of my day!!! Including double cream instead of the corn flour made a difference to the taste and creamier texture of the pudding and the starch released from the arborio rice did a great chemical job too. I love the 21st century and I still love my mum's traditional rice pudding; however, mine is ready within an hour with some strawberry syrup.

Osmanlieh

The origin of this dessert is unmistakably Turkey. Osman Pasha is one of the Ottoman rulers. The 'Osmanli' also refers to the 'Ottoman's Police or Soldier' who was practising power on the Lebanese people whether in the Mounts, Beirut or even Syria.

The dessert itself is made of long vermicelli threads, which are soaked with ghee, rose water and orange blossom water and rubbed in between the palms to make them softer and full of moisture. These vermicellis are then baked in vegetable oil as layers in the oven until golden in colour then stuffed with clotted cream and topped with fragranced sugar syrup. The 'Osmanlieh' also refers to the golden coin used through the Ottoman reign and this dessert is round-shaped and golden in colour just like the Osmanlieh.

This recipe is rich in its history and origin but also has the simplest flavours of crispy golden vermicelli that crunches into the smooth and fresh clotted cream. Aah, it is heavenly.

Ingredients

1x or 400g Pack of frozen Kataifi or Osmanlieh (found in the frozen section of many Middle Eastern shops)

100g ghee or unsalted butter

20ml orange blossom water

20ml rose water

50ml vegetable oil for each layer to be cooked in the oven (total of 100ml oil)

200ml sugar syrup (see page 164)

Method

1) Thaw the vermicelli threads and then rub it with the ghee or butter thoroughly to give it more moisture.

2) Add the fragranced concentrates (rose water and orange blossom water), and let it rest for about an hour in these flavours.

3) In the meantime, prepare the clotted cream (page 164) and allow to cool.

4) Bring two circular trays or moulds about 26 cm and add the vegetable oil; lay the vermicelli threads and pad them in nicely. Apply the same for the next tray and cook in the oven at 200°C for about 15 minutes or until deeply golden in colour and crisp.

Maamoul

Maamoul is a stuffed pastry, it comes from the word 'done' or 'made'. The dough mix does not require hard work, however the manual dexterity for stuffing the balls and then putting them into their moulds and baking them is the hardest of all. Usually, people buy the Maamoul from specialist shops and they serve them on Eids' day. In the villages, where it's hard to go the nearest city or where people have limited resources, Maamoul is often done the day before and sent to the local bakery to be baked in large trays.

Ingredients

5 cups fine semolina

1 cup coarse semolina

250g ghee butter

2 tbsp icing sugar sieved

½ tbsp instant yeast

1 tbsp Mahlab (Cherry stone spice – found in many Middle Eastern shops; just ask at counters)

30ml rose water

30ml orange blossom water

½ cup of water

Method

1) In an extra large bowl or stand mixer, add both types of semolina and apply the ghee into it. If using your mighty hands, rub the semolina against the butter with your palms until the mix is all even.

2) Add the sieved icing sugar, yeast and spices and water. Mix all well until they become like semi-soft dough.

3) Add the fragrant water and let it rest for about 24 hours. I remember my mum preparing the maamoul mix in the early evening and leave it in a cool dry place for the next day to start working on it.

The Stuffing

The stuffing can be made of three styles: the most popular and famous of them is that of the dates. The dates are usually pitted and minced into a paste mixed with butter to give it a shiny and smooth finish. Both rose water and orange blossom are added to this mix to enhance its flavours.

Date stuffing or Maamoul bil Tamer

500g pack of minced dates (found ready-made in Middle Eastern shops)

150g unsalted butter

40ml orange blossom water

40ml rose water

Pistachios stuffing or Maamoul Bil Fusutuq el Halabi

500g fresh unsalted pistachios, ground coarsely

150g caster sugar

40ml orange blossom water

40ml rose water

Walnut stuffing or Maamoul Bil Jawz

500g walnuts ground coarsely

150g caster sugar

40ml rose water

40ml orange blossom water

1) These are all mixed together evenly as it becomes like a stuffing and just placed inside the Maamoul dough then pressed into its mould and then baked in the oven.

2) Preparing 'Maamoul' is often associated with any 'Eid' or a feast day, it does not matter whether it's Ramadan, Christmas, Easter: people in the Middle East are always serving Maamoul.

3) All you have to do is make a mini ball out of the dough and then press it deeper into the palms of your hand.

4) Add your choice of stuffing, close the ball again and press it to your desired wooden mould, now tap on the work top and place in the baking tray.

5) Bake at 160°C for about 15 minutes or until slightly golden all around.

6) Once cooled sprinkle heavily with icing sugar if your choice was that of the maamoul with any of the nuts. If you are going for the one with dates then do not finish with icing sugar as the dates are sweet enough anyway.

Essential Hints

1) Line up your baking tray with parchment papers or just butter it all around.

2) There are several wooden moulds for maamoul: usually the round one for dates, diamond shape for pistachios and the dome-shaped for walnuts.

3) Always have extra flour on the side for the mould, to avoid the dough from sticking to it.

Cinnamon and Ground Rice Pudding (Meghli)

Meghli means 'boiling': it is obviously the boiling of the ground rice until it thickens with sugar and water. Traditionally, meghli is served in presentable ramekins or glasses and usually associated with the birth of a child or even as a celebration for any reason.

Puddings are certainly an old combination of ingredients. The Romans were experimental with their combinations. According to her book *Cooking Apicius,* Sally Grainger points out two similar puddings: almond and semolina pudding and the pine nut and honey pudding. Personally, I don't see why the recipes should not have evolved to be recreated during another time; where ground rice has been substituted with semolina and the flavours enhanced further with caraway and cinnamon.

Ingredients

8 cups of tap water

2 cups of caster sugar

1 ½ cup of ground rice

1.5 tbsp caraway

1.5 tbsp ground cinnamon

For Garnish

200g dessicated coconut

100g almonds (boiled, peeled and split in half)

100g pine nuts

100g semi ground pistachios (maybe bashed with your
pestle and mortar)

Method

1) Bring the water into a pot and put on heat, add the caster sugar
and stir until the sugar dissolves.

2) Add the ground rice and the rest of the sweet spices (caraway and
cinnamon) and keep stirring.

3) Keep the heat on medium until it starts to boil, keep stirring the
pudding continuously until it starts boiling and giving out bubbles.

4) At this point, reduce heat to the minimum while stirring
continuously; the pudding becomes thicker and thicker and more
bubbles start appearing.

5) Pour into little ramekins or onto a whole deep dish; let it cool and
garnish with the coconut and nuts. Meghli is best eaten cold after
being refrigerated for about 3 hours.

JUST DESSERTS

Strawberry Trifle

This is made of refreshing layers of plump juicy strawberries, tucked into it a layer of Madeira cake topped by a silky layer of crème anglaise (custard) and then some fresh whipped cream.

It is a traditional recipe of my grandmother who used to do it for us throughout Christmas; she never liked puddings as they were too sweet. She sometimes stored strawberries in the freezer and used them mashed up. My grandfather told me that trifles are originally English and they dated back to 1500s in the UK.

In honour of that, I salute you with this modest, modern and twisted simple trifle recipe.

Ingredients

3 egg yolks

284ml double cream

25g caster sugar

1 tsp vanilla extract

Zest of half an orange

300ml double cream (to be whipped for extra use on its own)

Loaf of a good quality Madeira cake (local food store)

200g fresh sweet strawberries (1 punnet)

Method

1) Separate the egg yolks and put in a bowl, add the sugar and vanilla, mix all together until they are light and smooth.

2) In a little pan bring the double cream into boil. Once it starts to boil add half of the cream into the egg yolk mix and fold them nicely together.

3) Bring them all back to a gentle heat and keep stirring until the custard thickens, but do not boil it.

4) Empty the custard into a bowl and let it cool.

5) In the meantime, whisk the double cream until thick and stiff.

6) Wash the strawberries thoroughly and cut into 4 pieces each.

7) Now you may test your patience and start assembling the trifle: assemble a layer of fresh strawberries, topped by crème anglaise, add a layer of Madeira cake then again some crème anglaise topped with some strawberries and then double cream.

8) You may do the above layers twice or even three times depending on the size of your service ware.

Orange Blossom and Crème Anglaise Pudding

This is my dad's favourite and simplest pudding. Every time I had a frown on my face he'd put a portion on my plate and tell me, 'Eat this Lina'. It is the absolute comfort food by my dearest dad.

Ingredients

5 plain croissants, nicely torn apart

1 pot double cream

4 free range eggs

1 pod of vanilla and zest of a lemon

100ml of full fat milk

175g caster sugar

1 bar of good quality white chocolate

40ml of orange blossom water

40ml of rose water

Hand full of raisins (optional)

Tiny bops of butter on the top

Icing sugar for final serving

Method

1) Tear the croissants up and place them in a round baking tin.

2) Sprinkle them with some of the orange blossom and rose water, also soak the raisins with the rest of blossom and rose water.

3) In a little pan bring the milk and double cream to a gentle boil on medium heat.

4) In the meantime whisk the eggs and sugar with a hint of vanilla and lemon zest and set aside.

5) The double cream and milk should have started to boil now, quickly break the white chocolate and remove from the heat and give it a quick stir.

6) Gradually add the mixture to the eggs and whisk until they are all mixed together.

7) Pour over the croissants gradually until they absorb it, add the raisins and the butter knobs all over.

8) Whack it in the oven on 180°C for about 25 minutes.

9) Take it out, sprinkle with some icing sugar and let it cool. *Et voilà*, just enjoy.

This pudding is traditionally Egyptian in origin and is known as 'Om Ali' (in other words; the mother of Ali). Originally it was made with bread soaked with milk and honey and some raisins; other versions made it with layers of puff pastry soaked with milk and stuffed with pistachios, almonds and walnuts and raisins.

My parents were successful leading business dealers; such a responsibility opened the doors of heavy international networking and the entertainment of guests. Obviously food at all levels from different parts of the world was practised in our home. I remember a funny little story from when my father hired our home chef. Our tributes go to the loyal Joseph, our best home chef, who allowed me into the kitchen to just try bits and bobs.

Father: So Joseph you know how to cook?

Joseph: Yes sir.

Father: So can you cook Lebanese or just African?

Joseph: No sir, I can cook everything. I am talented sir, my mother showed me how to cook 'Plassass' at home. [Plassass refers to stews with palm oil; they are absolutely delicious, by the way.]

Father: So Joseph what about Lebanese food? Sometimes we have parties and we need a lot of dishes.

Joseph: Don't worry sir, your Mrs can teach me and I will do it. You know sir I can cook anything; I can even FRY ICE.!!!!!

Father: Brilliant Joseph, you are hired and I need my Fried Ice dish on the table please.

Both my parents displayed excellent taste in product buying. My mum learnt the bread pudding or Om Ali from an Egyptian lady; however my father did not like the texture. My mum then substituted the puff pastry to croissants as this gave it a fluffier version. My father still thought there was something missing and he asked her to remove all the nuts and raisins and add crème patissiere. It actually worked and added another dimension to this pudding.

I came along and added white chocolate and some floral combinations to make it just different and even more divine.

Mousse Aux Chocolat

I love this recipe: it is simply rich, smooth, silky, airy and above all a delicious dessert that is passed on from my grandmother to my mum and now from me to all of you. Just do it.

Ingredients

(Serves 4-6)

3 large free range eggs

200g good quality dark chocolate (78%-81% mass cocoa)

3 tbsp caster sugar

1 tsp vanilla

Method

1) Separate the eggs and mix the whites on their own until stiff, add the caster sugar each spoon at a time while whisking.

2) In a bain marie, melt the bar of chocolate and in the meantime whisk the egg yolks until light. Now add them to melted chocolate (please be very careful and use a thick cloth as a bain marie is very hot) and whisk and set aside.

3) Add a dollop of the chocolate and egg yolk mix to the egg whites and fold gently from bottom to top; now add them all together and fold again.

4) Empty into desired cups or glasses and set in the fridge for about 2 hours.

5) Decorate with a squidge of whipped cream or a raspberry or strawberry with a sprinkle of sieved icing sugar, or even with half icing sugar and the other half with a sprinkle of sieved cocoa powder.

Petit Fours

Petit fours are an amazing and extremely popular French biscuit in the Lebanon. You may find it at any patisserie with a variety of flavours, colours and shapes.

It is certainly very popular in our family and I remember my grand-mother baking them for us at Christmas or as she used to say:

Lina, it's Noel and it's time for Petit fours!

She had a special manual shaper that my mum still keeps; unfortunately I can't get my manual dexterity around it so I use contemporary biscuit cutters. I love petit fours, they are softly crunchy and full of the vanilla flavour that just takes me back to our old kitchen in Beirut.

Today, I could not resist the fresh memory and decided to recreate it with my cutest princess, my Lameece who adores chocolate petit fours. I hope you cherish moments like this with your family members at home and bake this simple and amazing recipe.

Ingredients

425g all purpose flour (sieved)

150g corn flour, sifted

225g unsalted butter (room temperature)

100g icing sugar (sieved)

1 tsp vanilla extract

2 large free range eggs

Sprinkle of salt

70g of cocoa powder (optional to make the biscuits chocolatey)

Method

1) Sieve the flour, icing sugar and corn flour all together into a bowl, sprinkle the salt and combine the dry ingredients together.

2) Add the soft butter to the flour mix and start combining it. Add the vanilla and two eggs and knead until it becomes dough. If you are a chocolate fanatic then add the cocoa powder to the dough and work it all around until it becomes chocolatey.

3) Allow to rest for an hour and spread some flour on the work top and roll till it's thin.

4) Use your favourite shaped cutters and assemble in a baking tray on a parchment paper, bake at 180 C for 10-14 minutes.

5) Let the biscuits cool on a rack.

6) To assemble, spread some chocolate spread on one side and stick them together. My mother loves spreading apricot or strawberry jam and then finish with a dusting of icing sugar. However, I love melting dark chocolate and dipping the biscuits to it, then rolling it through dessicated coconut, coloured or chocolate sprinkles or even ground nuts. It is your taste and your own biscuit adventure. Just love it.

Sables (The Sand Biscuits)

Originally this is a thin shortbread biscuit – genuinely French. It originated from Sable-sur-Sarthe in Sarthe, Normandy. Sables can be flavoured with lemon zest, cardamom and ground cinnamon.

See recipe for the petit fours and just apply the ring cutter with a smaller ring used in the middle of the other pair.

Once cooled, spread your favourite jam, put them together and sprinkle some icing sugar with a sieve.

Sables are originally thinner biscuits than petit fours and usually slightly larger. They are enjoyed with a cup of tea or coffee. They come in varied shapes but usually the top shape has a little decoration on it, maybe a little circle, star or even a smiley face.

Tarte aux Fruits de Forêt
(Fruits of the Forest Tartlets)

Preparing the Pastry

3 ½ cups of self raising flour (sieved)

3/4 cup of corn flour (sieved)

1 cup of icing sugar (sieved)

1 pack of unsalted butter

2 free range eggs

1 tsp vanilla sugar

Zest of lemon is preferable to add some freshness

Method

1) Add all the dry ingredients together and rub the butter against them until the whole mixture is sandy in your hands.

2) Add the 2 eggs and start really kneading until the mixture becomes a steady and soft pastry that you can play with.

3) Rub your selected tart tin with unsalted butter, then place the dough and mould around the tin with no more than 1 cm of thickness. Use a tin foil on top of the tarte with baking seeds or some dried chickpeas.

4) Place in the oven at 180°C for about 12 minutes, take the tarte out and remove the tin foil and whack it in the oven for another 5 minutes.

Crème Patissierre

In a pan, add the following ingredients:

1 cup of full fat milk

80g unsalted butter melted or at room temperature

5 egg yolks

1 egg white

¾ cup sieved icing sugar

1 tbsp vanilla

Zest of a lemon

Method

1) Add the ingredients together in a pan. Heat.
2) Whisking, bring the mixture to the boil. Once boiling, reduce heat and stir that very quickly to avoid any lumps or burning.

Tartes are just great desserts and also among the many cakes introduced by the French colony to the Lebanon. The most popular is the Tarte au Fraise or strawberry tarte and many patisseries in Beirut compete with their best crème fillings; whether it's butter cream or patissiere or any other form of ganache.

The above is also my home creation. The tarts were baked in little tins and then built one on top of the other with a crème patissiere filling and fresh strawberries. I actually indulged this beautifully through the layers and enjoyed the textures from top to bottom unlike a straight one-layer tart. It all depends on how greedy you are.

Caramelised Cornflakes and Cream dessert

This is a favourite of mine and the kids. My mother used to make this dish for us when we were in Sierra Leone in West Africa. Both my sister and I were always caught in the fridge licking the caramel dripping on the fruits and cream. I believe you can opt for just strawberries and cream instead of the fruit cocktails; however in Sierra Leone we missed strawberries and all other berries so we used local ingredients.

Anyway just enjoy this dessert however way you like. *Bon Appetit!!!!*

Ingredients

500g cornflakes (original)
1x can of golden syrup
125g unsalted butter
300ml extra thick double cream
2x can of fruit cocktail

Method

1) In a pan pour the golden syrup and the butter. Let it reach boiling point and melt the butter thoroughly.

2) Put all the cornflakes into the mix, and stir them constantly and low heat.

3) Put them on a cake stand or any flat dish and make a circle with a hole in the middle.

4) Allow to cool for about 30 minutes, then put in fridge.

5) Beat the double cream till it reaches ribbon stage.

6) Drain the fruit cocktail, mix them into the whipped cream and put them into the hole made in the cornflake.

7) Serve a piece of the caramelised cornflakes with two scoops of fruit cocktail and cream. It is heavenly.

Coconut Cookies

This cookie is among the popular sweet snacks that one can buy from patisseries; they often come in large sizes. I remember it was sold in the school's shop in a little sealed bag. I never liked this cookie at all, I don't know whether it's the size or the excitement of other cakes in the shop.

When I joined my parents in Africa, my mum made this cookie for us at home and it was just scrumptious. I remember I was 11 years old and she allowed me to sip some Arabic coffee from her cup with the coconut cookie. Since then, I could not resist this cookie and it's always in one of my kitchen's jars. My kids adore it.

Ingredients

5 free range egg whites
150g caster sugar
250g dessicated coconut
1 tsp vanilla extract
Zest of a lime and an orange
Cherry glacé for garnish
Lemon rinds for garnish

Method

1) Place the egg whites into a bowl and the sugar, mix with electric mixer until the sugar dissolves and the mix is frothy with stiff peaks.

2) Add the coconuts, vanilla and citrus zest and give it another mix until all even together.

3) Place the mixture into a pan and heat for about 5 minutes while you're stirring from one side to another.

4) Let it cool for a minute or so. Grab a bit in your hand and make it like a ball, then pat slowly in your hand and place on parchment paper or in greased tray.

5) Tap with one cherry glacé and bake in the oven at 160°C for about 15 minutes or until golden brown.

6) Remove quickly and place in your desired box and let it cool there and then. Enjoy with a cup of coffee or on picnics.

Charlotte's Strawberry Mousse

One of the most enjoyable experiences is to eat a cake base topped with a layer of smooth and velvety mousse. Mousse has always been associated with chocolate in all its flavours; however, fruit mousse carries many recipes to a higher level of refreshment. This will definitely be a wow for your guests.

All you have to do is try this recipe to know what I mean.

This cake is made of three layers and involves couple of stages. My advice is to start a day in advance and make sure you have enough space in your fridge.

Cake Mix Ingredients

5 free range eggs

1 tbsp vanilla

Sprinkle of salt

Lemon and orange zest half each

150g caster sugar

70g flour

½ tsp baking powder

1 pack of sponge fingers

Method

1) Preheat the oven at 200°C and then reduce to 180°C at the time of baking.

2) Mix the eggs and sugar until dissolved. Add the vanilla and the zest of citrus.

3) In a separate bowl mix the dry ingredients together: flour, salt and baking powder.

4) Add the dry ingredients to the egg mix and give them another whisk for about 4 minutes.

5) Place in a round cheesecake mould rubbed with unsalted butter and some flour.

6) Put in the oven at 180°C for 30 minutes or until firm and springy.

7) Let it cool and start adding the sponge fingers tightly and neatly all around it. This is a bit critical as you may have to pull the edges of the cake slightly to fit the fingers in, but it will be worth it; it tastes heavenly.

Strawberry Mousse Ingredients

1x strawberry punnet (200g)

1x blueberries punnet (200g)

2 free range egg whites

Juice of half an orange

90g caster sugar

1 sachet of vegetarian gelatine

300ml of whipping cream

Method

1) Clean both berries with fresh cold water and soak in the orange juice and sugar.

2) Mix the whipping cream until it smooth and velvety, or until it gets to ribbon stage and place in the fridge.

3) Separate the whites from the eggs and mix until they form a peak: basically, until you can turn the bowl up side down and the meringue does not fall. This is an entertaining time for my kids as I let them do it.

4) Leave that to rest but not for long now, as you need to mix the soaked berries in a food processor or a hand blender and then sieve into a juice.

5) Take half the quantity of the juice and bring to boil, adding into it the vegetarian gelatine and give it a quick stir. Once it is about to boil, pour it back straight to the other remaining juice and let it set.

6) Fold the double cream into the egg meringue, then add the berry mix. Do not worry if the mixture falls apart a little bit as this a normal reaction, just fold until the mixture is all even and let it set in the fridge for about 3 hours or possibly overnight.

Glacage Ingredients

1x strawberry punnet (200g)

1x blueberry punnet (200g)

1 vegetarian gelatine sachet

50g caster sugar

Juice of half a lemon

Method

1) Clean the berries with fresh cold water very quickly.

2) Soak the berries in sugar and lemon juice.

3) Mix them with a hand blender or food processor until pureed, then sieve them from extracts and tiny grains.

4) Take half of the juice and bring to boil stirring in the vegetarian gel.

5) Pour back into the cold juice and let it cool a little bit, then pour over the mousse to form a sweet gelatinous layer and let it set in the fridge for about 2 hours. Then it's ready for final touches and eating.

Dry fruit Cake

This is a great fruit loaf enjoyed with my girl friends on a mid-morning with coffee or tea. It's also a great cake for picnics and will last for up to a week if not even more.

Ingredients

1 cup of caster sugar

1 pack of unsalted butter (soft)

3 cups of self raising flour

6 free range eggs

3 tsp baking powder

1 tsp vanilla sugar

Zest of fresh lemon

A glass and half of chopped dried apricots, sultanas, raisins and prunes mixed in ¼ cup of flour

Method

1) First and foremost preheat the oven to 180°C.

2) Using an electric mixer, whisk the eggs with the caster sugar until it melts thoroughly.

3) Add the pack of butter and keep mixing; it is preferable that the butter is at room temperature.

4) Once the butter is softly melted into the sugar and eggs, add the rest of the ingredients (baking powder, lemon zest and vanilla).

5) Last but not least, add the flour and fold them in nicely, continue whisking for about 8 minutes to make it smoother.

6) In a separate bowl, add the dried fruits; sprinkle them with some flour so that they don't stick together. You may now fold them into the cake mixture, stirring your wooden spoon in from the bottom, working your way up to the top.

7) Grease up your loaf tin with some unsalted butter and empty in the mixture. Place in the oven at 180°C for about 40-50 minutes or until it s thoroughly cooked.

Gateaux de Ananas (Pineapple Pudding)

I must admit, the gateaux de ananas is one of the favourite and most popular homemade cakes in Lebanese households. Ananas or pineapple in fact is used in many cake decorations and people enjoy its flavours.

Ingredients

1 pack of unsalted butter (250g)

5 large free range eggs

1 ½ cups caster sugar

2 cups of all purpose flour

1 ½ cup of orange juice and the zest

2 tsp baking powder

1 tsp vanilla extract

50g brown sugar

1x large can of pineapple slices

Couple of cherry glacé

Method

1) Into a bowl add the sugar and eggs; mix well until the sugar is dissolved and it is light and fluffy mixture.

2) Add the butter and carry on mixing, until all is well dissolved and the mixture is not lumpy.

3) Add the sieved flour and baking powder and mix all together for about 10 minutes. Now add the orange juice and vanilla with some orange zest and let it rest.

4) In the meantime, butter around a 26cm round tin, spread the brown sugar and place the pineapple slices evenly. Add the cherry glacé into each sliced pineapple circle and pour on the cake batter. Tap the tin couple of times on the work top to make it all even.

5) Bake in the oven at 160°C for about 50 minutes or until thoroughly cooked: use the cake checker.

6) Allow to cool and then flip over into your presentation dish.

Forêt Noir (Black Forest Cake)

The Forêt Noir is of German origin and known as *Schwarzwalder Kirschtorte* – literally meaning 'Black Forest cherry torte'. It is made of several layers of chocolate cake with whipped cream and cherries. Traditionally, Kirsch (a clear liquor distilled from tart cherries) is added to the cake; on the other hand the Lebanese add fruit juice.

Ingredients

250g unsalted butter

1½ cups of caster sugar

6 free range eggs

1½ cups of flour

3 tsp baking powder

4 tbsp cocoa powder

Zest of orange

1 tsp vanilla extract

200g fruit salad (canned)

Juice of the canned fruit salad

300ml double cream for whipping

Method

1) In a bowl mix the eggs with the sugar until it is light, creamy and the sugar has dissolved.

2) Add the softened butter and keep whisking until all is creamy.

3) In a separate bowl sieve the flour, baking powder and cocoa powder and add them to the creamy mix and carry on mixing until the batter is all evenly mixed.

4) Add the orange zest and vanilla extract. Give it another mix.

5) Grease the tin with a knob of butter, pour the cake mix and bake at 180°C for about 50 minutes or until its thoroughly cooked. Use the wooden skewer to check.

6) In the meantime, sieve the fruit cocktail and keep the juice to be used later in the cake.

7) Pour the double cream and whip until a stiff peak stage and leave in the fridge to cool and set.

Assembly

1) Cut the cake in half and allow to cool completely.

2) Add the juice of the fruit cocktail on to both layers of the cake to give it moisture and enrich its flavour.

3) Spread whipped cream all around the bottom layer, add the fruit cocktail into it and place the other half of the cake on top.

4) Spread more whipped cream to cover the whole cake and then garnish with some grated chocolate and fresh strawberries.

Cute Cheats

Basics

Pack of good quality vanilla cake mix
Pack of good quality chocolate cake mix

Follow the instructions and bake in a rectangular loaf mould. Once cooled completely cut equally into several layers.

Cream Spread

400g Nutella chocolate spread
200ml double cream to be whipped

Once the double cream is whipped, mix all together with the Nutella to give it a velvety consistency and allow to cool in the fridge.

Chocolate ganache for covering

400g good quality dark chocolate (87%)
200ml double cream

This is at the last stage, when the cake is completely assembled. The ganache is prepared and poured all over the cake and its sides continuously until all is well covered.

Assembly

1) Once the cakes are cooled, cut into different layers about 3cm thick and start by the chocolate layer. Spread some Nutella cream and then cover with a vanilla layer; spread with Nutella cream and then repeat until you have 4 or 5 layers.

2) Now turn the cake sideways: this to achieve a vertical stripy shaped look.

3) Prepare the chocolate ganache and let it slightly cool, pour over the cake and a with a table spoon you can make sure the extra ganache is settling on the sides as well. Repeat this until all thoroughly covered with a thick layer of the ganache and allow to rest in the fridge for about 2 hours before service.

Letter to the Lebanon

LEBANON, THE LAND of White, I miss you terribly and miss the days when I was in your arms. The war separated us and drove us away to other lands of the world.

This is aunty Dallal (my aunt's best friend), myself and aunt Samia, in the nearby bushes of Jbaa in the south of Lebanon.

I miss the beautiful and ever-white Sanine Mountain and the green reserves of the El Barouk mountains. On our way to the Mounts of Lebanon, we always stopped to buy fresh local produce from the community's farmers. They had herbal teas made of chamomile, aniseeds and other herbs; some locals were renowned for their honey and others for fruit syrups and jams such as blackberry, mulberry and rose syrup. A picture embedded in my head is the large stainless steel trays full of juicy plump peaches, excellent golden apples that tasted heavenly, grapes and pears.

The fresh springs of Jezzine and Jbaa (renowned villages in the South of Lebanon); cool afternoons where we go on walks to pick blackberries on the roads and some herbs from my aunt's best friend's gardens to make taboule.

My Jedo (Grandfather) enjoying Arabic coffee with my Grandmother. She is reading the cup for him; the people enjoy drinking coffee and sitting with members of family especially when they go to the village for summer holidays. This is their home in Jbaa, a good sized and famous village in the south of Lebanon.

The Casino du Liban and Piscine Aly are both top elite venues for functions and singers to entertain the Lebanese. Many world-famous singers performed in the Land of White: Charles Aznavour, Demis Roussos and Julio Iglesias sang at the Casino du Liban. I still remember the night when I went with my aunt for a concert of the Argentinian pianist Raoul Di Blasio in 1995. He performed the famous 'Hanna El Sekran' (Topsy Hanna) along side Mr Elias El Rahbani, one of the best Lebanese composers of all time.

The best songs and musicals that reflected Lebanon's history were composed by the one and only El Rahbani brothers and the famous singer Fayrouz, an angelic voice guaranteeing your journey around the universe as she sings her love lyrics, freedom poems and light-hearted folk songs. A voice that transports you to the galaxy, she is known as our ambassador to the stars.

I do miss the virgin villages of the Lebanon, a sense that was always expressed about by one of the best Lebanese writers, Khalil Gibran who wrote *The Prophet*. He comes from a beautiful village known as Bcharre in Northern Lebanon. I miss the days when people went out for walks in the late afternoon, gathered in the town centre and on Sundays danced the El Dabke, a traditional folkloric dance.

A memory that is deeply embedded from my childhood is the 'Kaak' man, usually an old man with a mini-wheel car that sold 'Kaak', a sesame ring bread that can be stuffed with zaatar mix or cheese. You may taste this 'Kaake' the modern way now at Abu Arab, a specialized shop selling 'Kaake' with new and creative flavours.

I miss the man with the pink candy floss car wheel: he had many pink bags but he was still spinning the candy floss fresh in his cart and all of us, children of that street, gathered around him to buy and enjoy the fresh taste of our childhood.

Beirut was lively; even as a city it was full of culture and had great traditions of love and sharing and people from different religions living together happily.

'Those were the days?' I literally do not want to accept this term anymore; I want my Lebanon back. I want it for all of us to share without any external interference, I want us fellow Lebanese to love each other again and stay together as we did in the golden days before the war ripped all of us apart.

What remains of Lebanon today is just ruins. Every year I visit this country with my kids and pick up on the memories that are not even there anymore. The people have changed; others fled for better opportunities. People don't enjoy themselves anymore but hey, there is one thing that is keeping us together and at least for now: it is the Lebanese jewel and that is our food heritage. So let's keep it safe and guard it in our own hearts. I hope that every reader safeguards their copy of this book and enjoys cooking and eating the Lebanese way.

My aunt Samia enjoying herself at one of the restaurants in East Lebanon, on our way to Baalbeck the Sun City in 1995. This shows how the Mezze (and Lebanese food in general) is: people enjoy themselves and share food on the table, dance and listen to folk music and have a good time. It summarises the essence of the Lebanese gastronomy inherited from the Assyrian banquets.

A man selling Kaak, with Picon cheese (spread cheese triangles) or with some zaatar, in the ancient city of Tyr (Tyre), south Lebanon.

This is my forever elegant Mum Fatima and my sister Maya. West Africa – Sierra Leone.

Cookery and Reference books

Dalby, Andrew & Grainger, Sally – *The Classical Cookbook*, The British Museum

Grainger, Sally – *Cooking Apicius, Roman Recipes for Today*, Prospect Books

Brothwell, Don & Brothwell, Patricia – *Food in Antiquity*, The Johns Hopkins University Press

Helou, Annisa – *Lebanese Cuisine*, St Martins Griffin

Apicius & Flower, Barbara & Rosenbaum, Elisabeth – *The Roman Cookery Book*, Martino Publishing

Conil, Jean & Marchbank, Richard – *Banquet Cuisine, Modern Banqueting Gastronomy*, Epicurean World Master Chefs Society